WORKING IN PUBLIC RELATIONS

Some other titles in this series

Applying for a Job
Buying a Personal Computer
Career Networking
Career Planning for Women
Coping with Self Assessment
Dealing with Your Bank
Doing Business on the Internet
Finding a Job with a Future
Getting That Job
Getting Your First Job
How to Know Your Rights at Work
How to Manage Your Career
How to Market Yourself
How to Master Languages
How to Return to Work

How to Start a New Career
How to Stard Word Processing
How to Understand Finance at
  Work
How to Work From Home
How to Work in an Office
Improving Your Written English
Learning New Job Skills
Managing Your Personal Finances
Passing That Interview
Starting to Manage
Surviving Redundancy
Using the Internet
Writing a CV That Works
Writing Business Letters

Other titles in preparation

The How To series now contains more than 200 titles in the following categories:

Business & Management
Computer Basics
General Reference
Jobs & Careers
Living & Working Abroad

Personal Finance
Self-Development
Small Business
Student Handbooks
Successful Writing

Please send for a free copy of the latest catalogue for full details (see back cover for address).

JOBS & CAREERS

WORKING IN PUBLIC RELATIONS

How to gain the skills and
opportunities for a career in PR

Carole Chester

How To Books

Cartoons by Mike Flanagan

British Library Cataloguing-in-Publication Data
A catalogue record for this book is available from the British Library.

© Copyright 1998 by Carole Chester.

First published in 1998 by How To Books Ltd, 3 Newtec Place,
Magdalen Road, Oxford OX4 1RE, United Kingdom.
Tel: (01865) 793806. Fax: (01865) 248780.

All rights reserved. No part of this work may be reproduced, or stored
in an information retrieval system (other than for purposes of review),
without the express permission of the Publisher in writing.

Note: The material contained in this book is set out in good faith for
general guidance and no liability can be accepted for loss or expense
incurred as a result of relying in particular circumstances on statements
made in the book. The laws and regulations are complex and liable to
change, and readers should check the current position with the relevant
authorities before making personal arrangements.

Produced for How To Books by Deer Park Productions.
Typeset by Kestrel Data, Exeter.
Printed and bound in Great Britain by Cromwell Press,
Trowbridge, Wiltshire.

Contents

List of Illustrations

Preface

Many people, young ones especially, perceive the world of public relations as among the most glamorous of careers. They probably think it's one long round of parties or tête-à-tête lunches with influential editors in the country's most luxurious restaurants.

In fact, there are humdrum aspects about the job: hours spent on the phone, on research, on paperwork and attending to fine details. There is no such thing as regular office hours since a PR may well have to be up at the crack of dawn for a breakfast meeting or exhibition and, just as easily, work well into the evening if an organised reception or product launch calls for it.

So be warned. At its best, public relations can be as glitzy as *Absolutely Fabulous* would lead one to believe, but at its worst it means long hours and hard work, often for little thanks.

Surprising as it may seem, given its popularity, public relations is still relatively misunderstood. The professionals will be very cross if you muddle its function with marketing, for example, though the two are allied. Potential employers are themselves not always aware of the true role of PR. In its purest and most useful form that role should be to advise, to have that advice accepted, then implement it and, hopefully, see some kind of beneficial result.

Advice may be part of the job, but it is not always heeded. During her life Princess Diana, for instance, did not always follow a PR's suggestion. What's more, while a public relations director (in-house or agency) should theoretically report directly to a chairman or chief executive officer, in many cases this is not so. It is, however, gratifying to know that increasingly the individual responsible for the PR function in major companies is part of senior management and that businesses are giving more recognition to that function.

According to the Institute of Public Relations (IPR), the formal definition of public relations is: 'The planned and sustained effort to establish and maintain goodwill and mutual understanding between an organisation and its publics.' The Institute, founded in 1948, is the UK's professional body for public relations, now with nearly 6,000 members, and intent on providing a professional structure for public relations practice. In recognition of outstanding work performed by members, the IPR awards fellowships.

What, though, of the way into PR in the first place? There are recommended qualifications, of course, as you'll read about in this book, but even the IPR admits that because so many different types of activities are embraced by a PR title, there is no set of ideal qualifications, nor any single route to take. Which is a happy thought.

If you have common sense, curiosity, flexibility, creativity, stamina and organising skills, public relations can be a most rewarding profession.

I should like to thank my many public relations contacts for their invaluable input, most particularly my PR guru and friend, Stuart Hulse.

Carole Chester

1
Introducing Public Relations

The field of public relations is something of a grey area. Few people truly understand it, including sometimes the companies which insist on a department for it. Nor are its effects always directly measurable, which can be frustrating for the person who wants to see a definite achievement. What's more, as a job title, it sometimes changes shades like a chameleon, which is why you may see job ads calling for Press Officer, PR Account Executive, or Publicist, among others. To add to the confusion, not all titles relate accurately to public relations, though all cover at least part of what it is.

> **At the core, PR is all about communications.**

That is why anyone with the right attitude can get into it. Indeed, being in the right place at the right time, with no specific academic qualifications, can prove just as fruitful as opting to take a course or degree.

DISCOVERING DIFFERENT ASPECTS OF PR

The aspects of public relations are as varied as the ways and means of getting a first foot in the door. Before deciding 'how', look at 'what' might be available to you, and for which aspect you are best suited. Writing, advertising, marketing and promotional know-how and skills, for example, can be valuable assets for the person intent on becoming a successful public relations executive, yet each of these fields is a career in its own right.

What are the main activities?

Some or all of the following activities could be involved in PR:

- programme planning
- writing and editing
- media relations
- corporate identity
- speaking
- production
- special events
- research and evaluation.

How are the activities defined?

According to the Institute of Public Relations (IPR), PR activities are defined as follows.

Programme planning
Analysing problems and opportunities, defining goals, recommending and planning activities and measuring results.

Writing and editing
Reaching large groups of people by the printed word. This might include shareholder reports, annual reports, news releases, film scripts, articles, features, speeches, booklets, etc.

Media relations
Developing and maintaining good working contact with the media. This involves applying knowledge of how all types of media work, as well as special interests of journalists.

Corporate identity
Developing and maintaining an organisation's identity via corporate advertising, presenting the company's name and reputation rather than its products.

Speaking
Communicating effectively with individuals and groups, including meetings, presentations and platform participation.

Production
Communicating by way of brochures, reports, film and multi-media programmes.

Special events
News conferences, exhibitions, facility celebrations, award programmes and competitions to gain attention of target groups.

Research and evaluation
Analysis and fact gathering to decide upon future strategy.

Starting with two distinct areas
Since many PR aspects are dealt with in subsequent chapters, this introduction will hone in on two very separate PR areas: customer relations and press relations.

LOOKING AT CUSTOMER RELATIONS

As the title suggests, customer relations involves direct dealing with the general public, often (though not necessarily) in face-to-face confrontation. In some instances the job title may be referred to as Customer Service, or in the case of a hotel, Guest Relations. Whatever the exact title, consumers frequently call for the person holding it because they have a problem. When this problem is as simple as 'When can I book a tennis court?', say at a resort, it is easily resolved. On the other hand, the customer in question may be extremely irate, perhaps because a guest room isn't ready or room service didn't turn up, and will need soothing.

Almost every type of company boasts a customer service department these days, from banking to BUPA, from department stores to train services. It is therefore the easiest aspect of PR to access, especially as a number of companies offer in-house training sessions once you have been hired; good news for the young, inexperienced jobseeker.

Before seriously considering this area, ask yourself the following questions:

● Do I like people?

- Am I good at calming someone down?

- Can I take verbal abuse without breaking down into tears?

- Am I a smiling person?

- Will I cope with answering the same old questions day after day?

- Am I polite at all times?

If you can answer yes to all the above, this may be a possible career path.

Choosing the best areas to investigate

Your biggest decision is whether you want to face the public in person, or merely converse with them over the phone. In the service sector (eg banks, insurance companies and other financial institutions), your work as a trainee will not involve seeing the general public, though as you advance up the ladder you may be asked, as a customer service manager, to train others, give seminars or attend conferences. So if you think you'll be happier 'voice-to-voice' rather than 'eye-to-eye', the following are among your best bets:

- banks
- insurance companies
- transport companies
- credit card organisations
- manufacturers of electrical goods
- utility companies.

If your preference is for public contact, a department store or hotel is a good choice. Remember that in the latter your desk will be right out front in the lobby. Remember, too, that a guest relations badge might mean organising activities for guests' children, as well as making sure flowers and wine are delivered to the correct VIP rooms. If you like the idea of direct visual contact, investigate the following areas:

- hotels/resorts
- airports
- department stores
- cruise lines.

Breaking into customer service
For the school leaver, there is really no set route other than standard school qualifications.

LOOKING AT PRESS RELATIONS

Press and public relations are invariably interlinked, especially in agencies. Theoretically a press and PR person should be a company or client **spokesperson**, as a link to both the departments as well as customer service ones, whereas PR agencies are not involved in customer service.

Breaking into press relations

Don't be deceived into thinking that a degree in public relations will earn you a top PR position immediately. Regardless of degree (of any kind), college leavers, like school leavers, can only hope for an assistant's post at first. Having said that, and because competition is particularly fierce in the PR arena, any of these help make you stand out of the crowd when it comes to shortlisting applicants:

- a PR or journalism degree

- any BA

- a diploma in business studies, media relations or as a secretary.

SEEING PR AS PART OF MARKETING

It may seem a little confusing, but PR frequently acts as an arm, or tool, of the marketing function. A company PR position may well be within the marketing department, reporting to a marketing manager or director. A Higher National Diploma (or degree) in marketing, therefore, is no bad thing. For school leavers especially, taking such a course could give them the edge when it comes to interview shortlists.

It is the marketing team that decides on the direction a product or service should take. While it is up to sales to 'sell' that direction, public relations backs up the strategy by publicising it.

Backing up marketing with PR

For example, Hotel X, which has just opened, is not quite in the centre of London. It is being marketed as a four-star product with value-for-money rates to match, but with an implied five-star service. Hotel X's PR must convey a positive message about its location and highlight its excellent quality and rate structure.

PR input to marketing

At the highest level a PR acts as the right hand of a company's chief executive officer, reporting directly to that person. Public relations input at this level can create direction and be part of decision making.

HELPING SALES THROUGH PR

Whilst it is the job of the sales department to sell goods or services on a profit basis, public relations can assist by increasing the demand and awareness.

For example, manufacturer Y has brought out a super-duper new toaster which does just about everything but make the bread, and comes in a wonderful range of colours and patterns. Any editorial about this new item that a PR can place will heighten consumer awareness and, most likely, demand. Sales will accordingly rise.

BACKING ADVERTISING THROUGH PR

Genuine PR is distinctively different from advertising, and purist consultants get heated when the suggestion is made that their work comprises obtaining unpaid advertising. Nevertheless, persuading the media to feature a specific item or service editorially is worth money to the client. Editorial, and in particular pictures, are actually considered worth more in financial terms than advertising. Consumers know an ad is an ad – mentioning only advantages – but will pay more attention to editorial which is perceived to be far more objective.

> Advertising and PR each have a message to relay – communicate – and often, therefore, work in tandem.

Backing up advertising with PR

Food company Z has launched a new range of vinegars, advertised on TV; that is a direct message telling a wide audience they are available. Thanks to subtle wooing by the company's PR, a national Sunday supplement runs a half-page feature on the choice and selection of vinegars, and in a comparison chart Company Z's comes first. This is an embellishment message, creating more subtle awareness. Those consumers who have seen the television advertisement are now given another objective reason for trying the product.

Remember, also, that some PR managers are given the additional responsibility of placing ads for their company or client's product or service. Media knowledge (readership status and circulation) is important in this case, along with the ability to utilise budget to best advantage, which may mean bringing negotiating skills to bear.

PROMOTING THROUGH PR

Whichever aspect of PR appeals to you, public relations is about promoting.

● Customer service/guest relations promote goodwill.

● PR managers/publicists promote products/services.

Promotion is so important that it has become a career title in its own right. Magazines, for example, have their own promotions department, involved in arranging reader offers and competitions. Manufacturers, particularly of foodstuffs, such as Nestlé, Cadbury or Schweppes, work with sales promotion agencies. Their job it is to dream up incentives and gimmicks to promote specific items and brands during a particular period. Sales promotion has become an 'industry' in recent years, and now requires youngsters wishing to enter it to take a Diploma (ISPND), but it is *not* public relations.

CASE STUDIES

Mark's customer service potential is spotted

Mark is well mannered, friendly, and has a pleasant telephone voice, but left school with only four GCSEs. He liked the idea of customer service and his enthusiasm for it was reflected in his letter of application to a major international bank, and further heightened when he was called for an interview for general bank employment. Although at a junior level, applicants don't know which departments they will be allocated to until they are accepted; department suitability is assessed during the interview. In Mark's case it was straight to the customer service department as a trainee.

Marianne gains the right qualifications and experience

Marianne graduated from university with a BA in English, but when she applied to a small London PR agency she had no work experience. She did, however, have the advantage of mutual friends of the agency's owner, and was taken on as a trainee. She is well spoken and well groomed, and in two years learnt a great deal about press relations. She has just been accepted by an agency double the size as account manager.

2
Working in an Agency

Agencies are frequently called 'consultancies'. Although the purists insist there is a difference, for the purposes of this book the two names are interchangeable. Either way they might comprise only one or two people, ten times that number, or even more.

The larger concerns have their own trade association, the Public Relations Consultants Association (PRCA), while individual PRs can be elected members of the Institute of Public Relations (IPR), whether they work for an agency or in-house. Both organisations have a code of practice.

In environmental terms, work in an agency is very different from that in a company, albeit that the type of work is probably similar.

ASSESSING THE PLUS FACTORS

Any PR agency worth its salt, even small ones, will be contracted to several different clients. As a greater number of clients is acquired, so an agency can grow – and employ more staff.

A newcomer at account manager or executive level is most likely to be hired:

● for specific product/service knowledge to handle a specific account of a type already familiar

● for proven work experience elsewhere

● or because they bring an account they have handled previously with them to their new agency employer.

A school or college leaver, on the other hand, is likely to be hired first as general dogsbody for several account managers. It's only later that they may be assigned to help just one or two, perhaps becoming one of an account team. If you consider yourself too much of a star to make the tea, answer phones or run errands, don't read on.

> **You can learn a great deal at junior level in an agency which will give good preparation for promotion.**

Whether a trainee or work experienced, if an agency (and its clients) like you and your work, they will want to keep you. One of the biggest plus factors, therefore, is that even if an agency loses a particular account, you are bound to be moved to another one.

Reputable agencies will offer you an employment contract, stipulating your rights to benefits and holidays, hours of employment, and expenses when appropriate. The best terms are more readily available at a sizeable agency.

Gaining wide experience

Since most agency account managers and executives are involved with more than one client, agency work is extremely diverse and can be more fun than that in-house. Even as a trainee you might be learning about, say, vitamins – and getting to know the pharmaceutical press and their needs – and wine – and getting to know the food and drink writers.

Should you be hired by a specialist agency, you have the opportunity to acquire specialist knowledge about a product or service type. For example, some agencies specialise in fashion accounts; others in travel or finance.

Summing up the plus points

● Regular employment with all benefits.

● Varied worklife, often different from day to day.

● Stimulating environment.

● Opportunities to get on fast due to rapid staff turnover.

WATCHING OUT FOR THE PITFALLS

Oddly enough, the plus factors of working in an agency can also be the pitfalls. Agencies pitch for accounts, and that means more than one agency will write a client **proposal**, coupled with suggested budget (if not already stipulated). Probably around three will be shortlisted, based on price, **presentation** and 'click' between potential client and proposed account manager. A contract, when achieved, may be for a short-term project, or for a year, after which time it will be reviewed. If the client is satisfied with the agency's work, the contract stands a good chance of being renewed; if not, it will go out to tender and may be won by another agency.

When an agency loses a 'big time' client, it obviously loses a certain amount of annual revenue. If it cannot replace that by taking on an alternative account, it may not be able to afford its number of staff. That could mean goodbye to some account manager, regardless how good their work. Although this is less likely to happen to a lower-paid trainee, who can be posted as help from A to B to C, it becomes a greater hazard the higher up the career ladder you climb.

Too many chiefs

Another pitfall is that within an agency there is more than one boss: the agency head plus the client. Underling managers and juniors must please both. In some cases the client is frustratingly finnicky, requiring several of its own people to vet and approve even a simple basic press release.

Summing up the pitfalls

● Account loss can cause staff cuts.

● More than one boss to report to.

Fig. 1. Flow chart of command in a PR agency.

CHOOSING WHICH TYPE OF AGENCY

Small and intimate agency

Because it is relatively simple to start up in business as a PR, there are numerous one-man bands doing this kind of work. They have often worked previously in a large agency, or are ex-journalists. Their business title usually includes their name, the word 'company' or 'and associates', (for which read assistance, either full-time or ad hoc). It is in the latter area that a junior has an opportunity to learn the ropes from an experienced professional PR.

Targeting the small agency
First ask yourself the following questions:

● Can I take orders from one person and do what I'm told?

● Would I enjoy working in someone's home?

● Do I enjoy menial chores like addressing envelopes and keeping notes?

If the answers are 'yes', then ask yourself:

● Do I, my family or friends, know anyone with their own PR business?

- Am I capable of secretarial work, and will I accept that this may be required as part of my training?

- Have I seen any newspaper ads for a junior assistant?

> **The easiest way to apply to join a one-man band is through friends or even passing acquaintances.**

The self-employed PR has particular need for secretarial and telephone help, but little time to teach you the wizardry of computers and word processors. So if you have that knowledge, emphasise it.

Medium-sized agency with opportunity
A medium-sized agency has undoubtedly grown thanks to success, and employs several staff.

> **When an opening occurs with a medium-sized firm, it is an excellent choice.**

Not only are you likely to work on several different accounts, but you'll also be considered very much a part of the team and in line for promotion.

Targeting the medium-sized agency
Ask yourself the following questions:

- Will I make a good team member?

- Am I prepared to listen and learn?

- Can I be patient about promotion?

- Do I consider myself a loyal person?

There's nothing to stop you writing on spec to any agency which might have a vacancy, if not this moment, sometime in the near future. But do your homework first. You can find out what PR agencies are doing, and estimate their size, by buying copies of

PR Week. This magazine publishes a league table of PR agencies in a supplement, usually around May each year. You can also visit your local reference library and ask to see the most up-to-date copy of a PR directory (*Hollis*), then make notes.

Large agency with high turnover
A large agency has made its name, quite often in a specialised sphere, and grown accordingly. Sometimes it is a result of a merger between two medium-sized agencies, or a takeover bid. Sometimes, too, it is the case of an advertising agency developing a public relations side to the business.

> **Although in some ways you are less likely to learn skills quickly, in other ways the bigger the agency, the better your chance of promotion since staff turnover tends to be high.**

Targeting the large agency
Ask yourself the following questions:

● Do I like a large office with lots of people?

● Will I mind jobs thrown at me from several people at the same time?

● Am I quick to see an opportunity to advance myself and grab it?

Although there is no sure way of knowing which is a large agency, if you have no inkling to start with, some of the larger ones tend to list themselves as 'group, plc, international', or with 'UK Ltd' in brackets after the company name. A list of the top UK consultancies is also published annually in *PR Week*.

MANAGING AN ACCOUNT

When you acquire an account of your own, you become the link between client and agency head, and are responsible for all work done on behalf of that client. Press enquiries about that

account will be directed to you personally, although there will
be stand-by support from account executive and assistant.

In an agency it is rare to control one account only, so you
will either log the amount of time you spend on behalf of a
client, or you will be told that you must spend a specified
amount of time, eg two, three or four days' worth of time a
week. This is because when agencies pitch for an account, they
promise a certain allotment of time in proportion to fee, and
costed on PR programme needs and objectives.

Keeping records

Keeping time sheets is essential, so that at the end of the week
actual time spent on an account can be compared with the
number of hours targeted.

After any meeting, either with the client or internal, a **contact
report** should be written up. This is like a secretary's minutes
and should list succinctly any decisions which were taken at the
meeting, as well as identify those individuals who will be
responsible for subsequent action.

Sample contact report
A fictitious agency called Carole Chester Associates has an
account for a destination called Silasia, for which Jeanne is in
charge, as account manager, assisted by Marie. After a meeting
with the boss of Silasia's London office, a contact report might
read like the one in Figure 2.

Targeting markets

Managing an account means you must be aware of target
'publics', ie: markets. There are bound to be several of them.
Take an example: A pharmaceutical company has brought out
a new multivitamin supplement aimed at the 50+ market. The
company produces a vast range of vitamin and mineral based
products suited to all age groups. What are its target markets
so far as a PR is concerned?

- trade (pharmacies and health stores)
- the health conscious consumer
- the 50+ consumer
- the young.

CCA   **CONTACT REPORT**

Client: Tourism Silasia

Subject: Tour operators/PR
No: 014
Date: 30/4/9x
Notes on meeting at Silasia House 29/4/9x

Present: Michael Wong (Tourism Silasia)
Tim Carsen
Derek White
Carole Chester
Also circulated to Jeanne Green, Marie Owen

1. *UK Tour Operators*	ACTION
Two senior tourism representatives from Silasia are due to visit London May 13–16. They wish to meet tour operators studied in the recent research. The following six were agreed: A, B, C, D, E, F.	MW
MW proposes that they meet with TS on PM of 14th May and visit the operators on 15th, 16th and 17th. An update on TS's contacts with the six tour operators will be prepared.	TS
2. *Publications*	
CCA has arranged a meeting with Z publications for 10.00 hrs on April 30th to discuss a supplement to Agency's July issue. We can also discuss 199x/x publications in general.	TS/CCA
3. *Media Visits*	
(a) The visit of ten writers to PAFTA via Barbican Airways will be nil cost to TS.	
(b) Five travel writers are going to Silasia June 6–13 (via Barbican Airways) to attend Silasia's international cultural festival.	JG

Fig. 2. Agency contact report.

A specialised media list takes priority here, so a PR manager will look at publications dealing with pharmaceutical products, good health magazines and the 50+ magazines. But in addition, and depending upon briefing and budget, the PR could find themselves involved in writing a booklet about the benefits of vitamins or organising seminars at schools.

Campaign possibilities

Managing an account can be extremely varied from client to client. Image could be a priority; research analysis might be necessary. Some PR campaigns are initiated to improve community relations, or those between the company and its employees.

For example, a tableware company has just bought out another well known brand of china. Its PR objectives could include:

● Publicising the fact of the takeover.

● Obtaining as much editorial coverage as possible of the company's move to new offices and introduction of new patterns.

● Giving PR support at an annual tableware exhibition.

Compare this with a 'go green' organisation's objectives, which might include:

● Organising presentations/talks on environmental matters at schools/social clubs.

● Arranging radio/TV interviews for the organisation's key personnel to raise awareness in the general public.

● Obtaining maximum coverage on the opening of a local complex which has won an environmental award.

GETTING AN ACCOUNT

This is the job of an agency director. It involves keeping ears to the ground to know which companies might be seeking agency PR, either for the first time or because they are unhappy with their existing PR help. Existing contracts also come up for renewal, at which time other PR agencies may well be invited to **pitch** for the account along with the current contractee.

The proposal

In some cases the total account budget is a known factor; in others a suggested budget is called for. In either case a **proposal** must be written and costed, showing what is being offered for a stated fee, and how client aims can be achieved. On occasion a proposal will be made after discussion with a potential client, to assess objectives thoroughly. Sometimes, however, an account is advertised with a free-for-all pitch before shortlist selection, but for which a proposal must still be made.

Normally, though, a proposal is only set out after a brief has been received: ie, what the client wants to achieve. Writing a proposal is a skilled task. It has to be concise, precise and yet sell that agency making it. Highlights will include:

● a summary (appreciation) of the situation

● recommendations for a plan of action

● realistic appraisal of the number of man-hours required to implement the programme

● identification of those agency staff designated for involvement.

Sample proposal
Suppose that the same fictitious agency (CCA) were putting in a bid for the Tourism Silasia account. What content headings would you find in their proposal? Figure 3 is an illustration of what could be expected.

PROPOSAL BY CCA FOR THE
TOURISM SILASIA ACCOUNT

CONTENTS

Introduction

The Incremental Year 199x/9x

Strategy in 199x/xx

Some Activity Points for 199x/xx

Level of Service

Budgets/Fees

Brief Facts About CCA

Fig. 3. Sample of an agency's proposal.

Budgeting

Budgeting is a much greater bugbear for an agency than for an in-house PR department, since office overheads and everyone's salaries must be taken into consideration as well as a profit margin. The agency must recover all costs of materials supplied on behalf of the client, such as stationery, postage, printwork and photographs. Travel and entertaining expenses must also be recovered.

STARTING YOUR OWN AGENCY

Many account managers evolve such a good personal relationship with the client that they are tempted, and may be able, to take the account with them should they move to another agency or set up on their own.

Starting up your own agency is simple enough providing you

have done your homework on costings. For more about this, see Chapter 6.

CASE STUDIES

Stuart explains the benefits of a small agency

Stuart Hulse has run a successful public relations business for twenty-five years, at one time employing as many as twenty-five people in the agency bearing his name. Although he sold his large agency a few years ago, he loves the PR field too much to quit it. Now he still runs his own show with a few choice clients and an assistant.

After being trained up by him for two years, his last (university graduate) assistant was head-hunted by a medium-sized agency to act as account manager. His most recent recruit is also a graduate (with a degree in art). Stuart's own specialism is in the tourism and travel sector and his own career began in journalism. Although he works out of a centrally located office, in many instances self-made PRs operate from home.

He says: 'Like most PRs, I am inundated by letters from school leavers seeking employment. To hire a trainee these days, I would expect them to have a degree (to show a discipline for work and learning), although in my opinion it doesn't have to be a related one. Letter and CV presentation is important, but so, too, is personal appearance. I would not consider a person who is not well spoken or turned out. Personal recommendations are useful – my current assistant was recommended by my former assistant who knows her well.

'On the spot training stands a young person in good stead to excel at their career. I feel that someone would gain a great deal from working for an experienced PR – something that really cannot be learnt in school, but I would expect a college leaver to stay a minimum of two years, both for their own benefit and mine.'

Ann knows what a medium-sized agency needs

Ann Garland and her partner have run a business venture together for some years and employ about eight people. They consider themselves on the smallish side of a medium-sized agency and expect trainee staff to show loyalty.

'I expect a covering letter in addition to a CV . . . sometimes it's a giveaway to whether the sender is worth interviewing. Personally, I don't like the kind of letters which tell me how great the writer would be for my business, and a line goes straight through those whose content obviously shows they have done no homework on our type of company.

'We believe that if we invest time in a school leaver, there should be some return on that investment. We did hire a graduate a while ago on the understanding that we would give the training and she would give two years' of her time. She left after only one year which we didn't think was on. Our most recent recruit has a journalism degree. His course involved some work experience on a local newspaper, which we consider ideal.'

Ann's own career background is based on hotels.

Jenny describes work in a large agency

The Shandwick Group is the result of several mergers and takeovers. Today the Group employs thousands of people in a broad range of PR disciplines that include financial, technical, corporate and leisure. One of the companies which Shandwick bought was TPS, in 1990. Jenny Crayford worked for TPS for fifteen years, ending up on the board. Today she still works part-time for Shandwick.

Jenny says: 'Working in an agency is stimulating because no two days are the same. You have support from colleagues and are able to talk through ideas. Like many agencies we take on young people for work experience, either straight from school or post-graduation. Only pocket money is paid and anyone too grand to make the tea or photocopy material should not apply, but those who show keenness and enthusiasm during the work experience time with us are generally offered a proper job subsequently. It's a question of if the face fits and enthusiasm. We generally have three trainees who spend a couple of weeks with us at holiday times; post graduates might spend a couple of months.

'No trainee (even those with a degree) can expect to walk in the first day and write a relase, so work is pretty menial at first. But extra hands are always needed in an agency of our size, so eagerness will be rewarded. If someone applies as account executive, we would expect them to have some experience. We look for particular talents – the ability to write or having worked for a company in some capacity.'

Her advice is to telephone, send in a letter and CV and follow up with another telephone call if you are planning on the work experience route.

SUMMARY

If you work in an agency, be prepared:

- for myriad changes

- to learn and adapt quickly

- to handle time-management and budgeting

- to work in a team.

3
Working In-House

Working in-house means working exclusively for one particular company. Large organisations often boast a press office or corporate affairs department where several people are employed. Smaller, or private companies, may simply designate one person to perform a PR duty. It is possible, too, that a company makes use of both in-house PR and an outside agency, in which case the latter will report to the former.

Because the in-house PR is on the spot, access to information or personnel is that much easier. Fingertip, factual knowledge is an asset should a news story break.

In addition to the type of work that an agency might be called upon to do, the in-house PR department might also have to concern itself with internal PR and/or in-house literature.

ASSESSING THE PLUS FACTORS

It is reasonable to assume that a professional public relations executive can operate efficiently for any company, but if you genuinely believe in that company's efforts or products you'll inevitably perform a better, more credible job in terms of promoting those products or services.

> One of the biggest plus factors of working in-house is precisely because you love it, you want to be part of the company team.

You'll be providing a full-time service, not based on man hours, though obviously time management of your day remains an important consideration. You will also gain more in-depth knowledge about the company's affairs than any agency could ever achieve.

Gaining benefits and facilities

Benefits are another big plus factor. On the whole, major companies at least, offer much better employee terms than most agencies. Fringe benefits are likely to include:

- a car
- an expense account
- paid maternity leave
- sometimes creche facilities for those with small children.

Employee facilities can be an extra boon: social clubs, recreational programmes, office canteen, to name three. Depending upon the type of company, perks can include discounts on whatever the company offers, for example, savings on hotel rooms, airline tickets, money off apparel or household goods, lower mortgage percentages.

Gaining job security

There is also a greater sense of permanence. Unlike an agency for whom accounts come and go with irritating regularity, the in-house 'account' is always there. Of course, you could lose your job through inefficiency or corporate takeover, but the company which has relied on public relations activity, internally, in the past, is likely to continue to do so.

Summing up the plus points

- Feeling part of a team.

- First class terms of employment.

- Fringe benefits.

- Perks.

- Social environment.

- Greater permanence.

- Thorough product knowledge.

WATCHING OUT FOR THE PITFALLS

The biggest plus factor may be the biggest pitfall, for you can become so wrapped up in company 'selling' that you eat, sleep and drink it, with little time or energy left for any other part of your life. An in-house PR might well become so fanatical about what he or she is promoting that they lose objectivity.

Retaining objectivity and maintaining awareness of the competition, which should be bywords, often slip from reach. It is more difficult to see situations impartially from inside a company than outside it, which could damage credibility with the media.

Becoming narrowly focused

Unlike work in an agency, your channels of interest will be restricted to those which relate to the company, ie dealing only with a specialised section of the media or only certain PR activities. Narrow knowledge may or may not be to your benefit should you desire to change jobs.

Lack of diversity could lead to boredom or lack of challenge. Agency PRs frequently claim that their in-house counterparts have to do the same old things day after day.

There is also the pitfall of running into a career cul-de-sac. Once you have acquired the top company PR/press officer status, where do you go within the company? In an agency, on the other hand, you can climb the ranks to managing director, partner, buy it out or start your own.

Large organisations seeking a PR executive frequently demand an applicant with several years' experience. School leavers will therefore have a harder task getting their foot in the door of a company than an agency.

Summing up the pitfalls

- Becoming a company fanatic.

- Losing objectivity.

- Becoming an introvert or narrow minded.

- Job experience needed first.

- Potential career cul-de-sac.

- Possibility of boredom.

CHOOSING WHICH TYPE OF COMPANY

Choosing which company to apply to will depend on your likes and dislikes and your qualifications, as well as job availability. In order to keep it simple, it could be said there are three main areas or types of industries you could consider working for:

- leisure
- goods
- services.

Looking at leisure

The leisure industry is perceived as one of the most glamorous areas, hence the most fiercely competitive for entry. It is, however, a vast and varied industry, with abundant PR opportunities. Among the main sectors are:

- hotels
- airlines
- cruise lines
- tour operators
- destination attractions
- tourist boards
- film and TV
- restaurants
- sport.

Targeting the leisure industry
Former airline stewardesses, hotel reservationists, secretaries, pursers and entertainers have all been known to move into PR

within the leisure industry, once again proving no career access path is set in stone. Nevertheless, qualifications are valuable. Marketing courses, travel and tourism courses and catering courses can help to open doors. The IPR has control of the PR side of the Communication, Advertising and Marketing Education Foundation (CAM), so a CAM diploma should not be dismissed, while PR is a second-year subject for the Cranfield School of Management's MBA programme. Check out the London Chamber of Commerce and Industry's PR exams, and also those given by the Association of Business Communicators.

Leisure industry 'musts'
For leisure industry PR the following attitudes could be helpful:

- sense of humour
- love of fun
- adventurous personality
- sporty streak.

What's good about goods

'Goods' may mean specific types of products, tableware for example, in which case this is an ideal area to acquire specialised knowledge. Goods may, however, cover a broader and far more diverse range, as in the case of department stores when no two days' work will be alike. Among the main sectors are:

- department stores
- supermarkets
- manufacturers
- publishers.

Targeting the goods area
How do you gain access to these industries? The answer is very similar to that for the leisure industry: no one way. Start by asking yourself if you have any related knowledge. Summer work in a department store or supermarket, for instance, will have given you some idea of how those operations run, or if you've written a book you'll have an inkling of how publishers publicise material.

Goods industries 'musts'
Ask yourself if you have the following attitudes:

- product concern
- love of design
- precise nature.

Serving services
Services refers to those areas which serve the public. Many of them are linked to finance, but this sector also includes local government bodies, national or regional concerns such as water boards and Social Services. Among the industries to investigate are:

- banks
- insurance companies
- other financial institutions
- utilities
- local government organisations.

Targeting the service area
Perhaps more than any other, the services area may require well defined, specialised experience (see Chapter 8). Were you to enter a financial institution, for example, a solid knowledge of financial PR would be a great asset. The service area is often more sensitive than others and without the ability to handle crisis management, you are unlikely to be hired. Even so, providing you do have sufficient sound business knowledge and PR experience, the services area of PR can be the best paid of all.

Service industry 'musts'
Ask yourself if you have the following attitudes:

- logic
- managerial mind
- business know-how.

Internal PR

As an in-house PR, you could well be as much involved with company employees as you are with outside media. Indeed, you may have been specifically hired to handle internal affairs. You could be part of the board and therefore have a major role to play, or you may more simply be responsible for internal relations for a specific company segment. Perhaps you will be in charge of an in-house magazine or newsletter; possibly you will be required to write speeches for the chief executive. Maybe you'll be asked to oversee community relations or organise incentive schemes.

House journals

Call it what you like – company newspaper, employee news-letter, house journal – the in-house media can play a vital part in a company PR's job. If you are designated to edit such literature, you may be required to give a news digest to employees or publish features about certain employees. You might include other more commercial special offers and articles of interest to the staff.

It will be up to you to organise photo shoots of (locally) newsworthy events but, given the budget, you might well hire journalists to perform the writing tasks on a retainer basis. If you are not contracting out completely, your knowledge of print and design will be useful.

Sometimes, of course, what is basically thought of as an in-house journal actually has a far reaching audience. Think of airline and hotel magazines, for instance. Most of the latter companies negotiate a contracted deal with a publishing house, which still allows them to oversee the project and add a few pages of their own.

UTILISING PRODUCT KNOWLEDGE

Before you decide on which companies to apply to, write yourself a list of products you know about. Perhaps your hobby is tinkering with cars or perhaps you're a whizz at computers. You could love collecting interesting china, glass or antiques or you have a 'feel' for fabrics. Alternatively, you possess a fine-tuned palate for wine or food, or perhaps your friends think your colour sense is unparalleled. Any of these talents could prove valuable to certain companies.

PROMOTING A PERSON

Strictly speaking the 'publicist' is not usually an in-house PR, though if you are hired by a very well known celebrity who is demanding your exclusive time, it is virtually like working in-house. Promoting such a person requires care: too much publicity at one go could result in overkill; publicity of the wrong kind could harm image. On the other hand, if a book is due to be launched, the publicist would want to dynamite the media for coverage of both book and author prior to release date. Similar efforts are needed for new films.

A PR often uses the phrase 'raising the profile' of a person. Frequently, that person is a government minister, union official or similar. Among the PR tricks of the trade to raise profile is preparing articles on appropriate topics (such as law or environment) and placing them in appropriate publications under that person's name.

You may care to note that advertising sometimes uses that 'raise the profile' approach to promote a service . . . think of Peter Davis in the TV commercial for Prudential, The Man from the Pru.

CASE STUDIES

Eric finds satisfaction in in-house leisure PR

Eric Flounders has been in charge of public relations for Cunard in the UK and Ireland for fourteen years. Prior to that he was with Rank's leisure division, though he started his career life as a geography teacher.

He says: 'In an agency you get landed with a different account every month and never really feel on the inside. What you need to know tends to drift to you *ad hoc*, which is not very satisfactory. In-house you are in greater control, can do more things, work out a strategy for yourself and so drive things along.

'Much of what I do is generate positive feature material rather than news or fending off press enquiries. I accompany some press groups on trips, though some journalists may travel individually. Such exercises are designed to keep Cunard in the public eye in the most positive way possible, which is easy because I believe the product is good. Believing in the product is essential to do a good job.

'To work in-house you've got to be organised, keep records so you know what you said two weeks ago, be systemised. Maybe you do run the risk of losing objectivity, but I don't think that matters – it really is enthusiasm which counts. I'm honest about any product faults – that's my style – and it's no good pretending there isn't a problem if there is one. It's how you acquire the balance with the positive, good things.

'Doing PR for the QE2 is a gift. The only time my job becomes difficult is when minor things become page one stories, because the ship is so newsworthy. I might well have people call me up in the middle of the night just for a confirmation the ship is three hours late. If this grants a piece on page one, then that's the downside.

'There are now three of us in the PR department, as well as an outside agency. One of the assistants was chosen because she had worked on ships preparing daily programmes so knew a lot about the cruising side. I would not necessarily look for a junior with a PR degree, but rather someone with a certain personality – and I don't mean one of those gushing, Alice-band type of people who would drive most news journalists to distraction. They'd need to have a brain and a lot of common sense and be able to react sensibly under pressure.'

Valerie's in-house goods PR needs in-depth knowledge

Valerie Baynton has held the position of press officer for Royal Doulton for the past two years, but she has been that company's employee for thirteen – as curator of Doulton's Museum and handling factory tours. She says: 'There was an element of PR in this because I quite often communicated with the press, having all the historic information. Indeed, I took a university degree in medieval and modern history and an MA as well.'

For Valerie, her degree gave her advantages for this kind of in-house job. She points out: 'Although I am giving the media current product information, I also know the company history and how products are made, which helps what I do. Experience and knowledge of a company allows a PR to do a job more effectively. There are many aspects to this job, including the licensing division, and the hotel and airline division. Each division has different needs so requires a different response.'

Valerie reports directly to the PR director (concerned with internal affairs as well as external) and has one secretary to assist. 'Doulton would consider a junior for this department, not necessarily a degree holder, but one with communications ability who could give some indication of training or experience. I believe a history qualification does give ability to write, for example, even if the person had no specific work experience.

'If there is a downside to working in-house it is perhaps that sometimes you can't see the wood for the trees. You are so in tune and in touch with the company you work for, you may not have fresh ideas that could be instigated from other areas.'

Peter knows the needs of in-house service sector PR

Peter Jones has been in PR for twenty-five years, much of which was spent working for British Airways. A few months ago he joined BUPA as director of corporate communications, reporting directly to the chief executive officer. He started off his career life in journalism, taking courses on local government, law, current affairs, etc on block release under a three-year indenture contract with NCTJ.

Peter joined what was then BOAC because he wanted to stay with the media but had also achieved business and management experience. He says: 'When you work in-house you are closer to the problems and issues. In a consultancy you can never get that close. In an agency, you tend to get spread too thinly over a number of diverse clients unless you are a specialist. Each client thinks they have bought you body and soul. If there is a downside to working in-house it's the possibility of choosing an area which ultimately doesn't interest you, whereas in a consultancy you can move to a more amenable account. Some people would say the downside of working in-house is the lack of variety.

'I have always enjoyed the varied aspects of travel so BA was perfect as it involved engineering and aeronautics as well as the holiday and business travel factors. In BUPA there used to be a

PR department handling the media, as well as an internal communications department plus a government affairs effort – the ultimate result was it was somewhat difused. Now those three areas have been brought together into one department, represented at board level.'

The other twelve people in the department report to Peter, but new recruits must have experience. 'I prefer people with some journalistic background like myself. That's because you speak the media's language and know their needs. This is especially important if the company you're concerned with has a high media profile.'

SUMMARY

Working in-house offers the following potential:

- diversity of company types

- broad range of PR activities

- great depth of knowledge

- possible board-level status.

4
Learning the Basics

Servicing the media is a major part of a PR's job. Getting to know – and understand – the media does require more than a conversation over a gin and tonic. Happily, however, there are some easy-to-grasp basics for the beginner.

KNOWING HOW THE MEDIA WORKS

Realising publication deadlines
It is surprising to find too many so-called 'communicators' remain unaware of the way in which publications work, and haven't got a clue about deadlines. PRs who present a story about an event happening in two weeks time to a monthly women's magazine should not be amazed when coverage is turned down. Most women's magazines work to a three to six month advance editorial schedule. By the time they can allocate space to cover an event, that event may be over.

There is a way round this, if the occasion in question is an annual happening and providing the client knows there will be almost a year's wait before editorial appears. You inform/invite a particular member of the media about/to the event to make them aware of it, and in the hopes they will publish a piece in advance of the next annual happening. Bear in mind this can be a problem for an agency: by the time the event is given media coverage, a different agency may be involved, so *your* kudos could go out the window.

Similarly, a PR with a news story for a weekly trade paper should ensure it is mailed, biked, faxed or E-mailed before the day that publication goes to press. By the following week the story could be 'dead' or a more topical story takes precedence.

> **Always make sure of right timing.**

Mailing musts

Living in the world of electronics, the need for mailed printed material to journalists will undoubtedly diminish. Even now faxed material is beginning to supplant that in the post. A word of caution: many of your target press will be freelance and, whether or not they have E-mail *and* fax machine, are unlikely to want to see either facility crammed with unwanted information. Phone first.

Sending photos

At the moment, too, photographs (as opposed to CD Roms) are still finding their way to editors' desks. Make sure you:

- always back the picture with card

- or use a jiffy envelope

- never attach a compliment slip to it by way of a damaging paper clip

- phone before faxing

- protect pictures.

Telephone test

If you're calling up a journalist to invite them to a reception/ product launch/trip, don't immediately follow it up with 'What do you do?' or 'Who do your write for?' If you don't already know, why are you calling them in the first place? Juniors and secretaries should be briefed properly before being asked to make such telephone calls. This situation has happened many times to this author, with the result the PR in question (often an agency) doesn't rate very highly. To sum up:

- do your homework.

WRITING A PRESS RELEASE

Writing a **press release** well is probably the biggest basic of all. Rubbishy releases merely get binned, never printed. They are often too long, sent too late, use too many flowery adjectives and not enough facts, or are simply not target-marketed correctly. That means: waste of time, waste of money.

It stands to reason that the person with even partial journalistic skills will find it easier to compose a press release than someone who has difficulties stringing words together in sensible order. Even so, there is a knack and technique to press release writing which can be learnt.

Despite what some professionals might have you believe, there is no specific style to presentation of a release, privided that:

● sentences and paragraphs are kept short

● there is plenty of margin space and space between paragraphs

● headings are kept crisp and to the point.

Creating a news release

Journalism trainees on the hunt for news items have long been told to ask the five Ws:

● who
● what
● where
● why
● when.

PRs attempting to write **news releases** should remember the same rule.

Providing news, like PR itself, is providing information. That information doesn't have to be brand new to be of interest, if it has been hitherto unknown. Nevertheless, pay attention to publications' deadlines. Remember what is news today, is history tomorrow.

The opening paragraph should be eye-catching, it may be all

an editor reads. For eye-catching, read 'factual'. Give the gist in the first few sentences and a recipient may read on for further details.

News doesn't have to be a page-one block buster. In its simplest form, it relays information that a new hotel/restaurant/attraction has just opened; that the world's biggest mega-liner is being built; that a soap star has been awarded an MBE.

Summing up
Ask the following questions:

● Have I got news to tell?

● Is the main point in the first paragraph?

● Have I used too many adjectives?

● Have I included all 'must' information?

● Is the release not too long?

● Have I dated it?

● Have I put a contact name and number on the bottom?

If you can truthfully answer yes to all the above, you are certainly on the right track.

Writing other releases
There are several different types of release you may be required to write. Among the most likely are the following:

The backgrounder
Putting together a press kit often requires inclusion of a **background release,** a company history perhaps, or an updated report on market trends in a specific sphere. This should be designed as file information for a journalist to hang on to.

Such background releases, by their very nature, are likely to be substantially longer than the news release.

Example of good opening paragraphs to press releases

Luxury global group Concorde Hotels has increased its presence in the UK with the addition of the four-star deluxe Westbury Hotel, bringing to four the number of member properties the French-owned group has in the capital.

*

The Second World Summit on Television for Children is heading for the Queen Elizabeth 11 Conference Centre, from 9–13th March, 199x. The Summit's aim is to encourage the production of quality children's programming throughout the world and will bring together 1,000 delegates, including leading broadcasters, producers, politicians and academics to witness over seventy international speakers.

*

Beaches Negril is offering holidaymakers the most comprehensive Suite Concierge Programme in the Caribbean. Effective October 1 199x, Beaches Negril will expand its Suite Concierge Programme to include the Beachfront One Bedroom Suite and the Beachfront Two Bedroom Suite.

In all the above, the first paragraph has encapsulated the gist of the whole release. By comparison, look at the following illustration:

Example of a bad opening paragraph to a press release

Get away this autumn to a land of romance and intrigue, the landmark Hyatt Regency Pier Sixty Six resort in Fort Lauderdale.

The above actually says nothing, and it is only with paragraphs three, four and five that the recipient reads information of special packages this resort is featuring.

Fig. 4. Good and bad press release intros.

New appointments
New appointments should not be made into a meal if they're a mouthful. Very few publications allow space for more than a change in title or company, with perhaps one additional sentence relating to the subject's age, marital status, background or hobbies.

Features
Feature releases are designed to be printed more or less as they are, and are generally aimed at provincial papers and magazines which lack sufficient time and staff for re-writes. They should never run over two pages and should not refer to the company or product represented more than twice.

Sometimes the media will accept an article written by a PR if it is authorative and themed. In this case, a particular publication must be targeted and will have exclusive use. It could behove a busy agency PR to hire a freelance writer to put such an article together, once the agency has negotiated with the magazine and ascertained that it is interested in a certain topic and will guarantee inclusion if the article lives up to its 'sell'. The PR pays the freelance writer for his/her contribution, the magazine doesn't, but the PR benefits from knowledge that the story will run in a forthcoming issue.

When you are proposing a feature for a specific publication, make sure you ask the following questions:

● number of words required
● copy deadline
● any illustrations
● any special treatment
● issue in which it will appear.

Embargoes
Sometimes you may have to put an *embargo* on your press release, but only if your advance information to the press warrants it, say a VIP's speech which has yet to be made. Be careful before you decide on an embargo. For example, you may have good reasons for not wanting the media to use information until late in the day, but Breakfast TV wants to use the story at the start of the day. Do you take off the embargo and maybe

kill that later press coverage, or reckon the television report will actually increase media interest? This is a tricky decision to make, so do it with care.

Mailing lists
Mailing lists are all-important. It is often worth the effort of compiling separate mailing lists for different types of release. With experience, you will also get to know which publications are most likely to use your releases. Remember, too, there are news agencies such as PA and Reuters to which newspapers subscribe and therefore may be worth mailing. Bear in mind that newsy snippets and/or captioned photographs are of more interest to such agencies than reams of information.

HANDLING PRESS ENQUIRIES

If your client or company is a well-known and newsworthy concern, there will be plenty of telephone enquiries for information and photographs. When you respond quickly and efficiently, you stand a good chance of building up excellent rapport with journals that are beneficial. The greater the rapport and the more professionalism you show, the more likely the journalist will approach you first.

If you are new to an account or company, or the organisation you represent is new itself, it is always a good idea to appraise the press that you are available to give out information. PRs who are the most obliging will find they receive future enquiries.

Some press enquiries will stem from the fact that you haven't included sufficient details on a press release; a waste of your time that you could have prevented. Some enquiries come about because a press release has sparked a writer's interest, to your advantage.

Pressing for advantages
Printed material continues to give more in-depth coverage than broadcasting and since it can be carried anywhere should not be thought of as the media's dinosaur. Glossy magazines are read by far more people than those who originally buy them – think of the hairdresser's or the doctor's waiting room. They

also stick around beyond their sell by date, another extension of readership.

While the professional PR will always respond to any press enquiry, it is wise to evaluate the enquiry's source. Most people think coverage in a national newspaper is the bee's knees, but the daily has a shorter life than a monthly magazine. On the other hand, one paragraph in the popular press can be far more valuable than a two-page spread in a specialised magazine.

Points to remember

- Circulation is not readership.

- Niche market journals may be worth a goldmine.

- Print media may be just as effective and certainly less costly than TV.

UNDERSTANDING THE MEDIA

There are three main sorts of media:

- print
- radio
- TV and film.

Print

In the UK there is national and regional (provincial/local) press. A national readership survey's figures can be useful to the PR looking to evaluate its media coverage. Newspapers can be:

- national dailies and Sundays
- regional dailies, evenings and weeklies.

Magazines can be:

- consumer-led
- trade or technical

- weekly
- monthly
- bi-monthly
- quarterly
- or annual.

There are also many free broadsheets and magazines, door-dropped on a local basis.

Benn's Media Directory profiles publications, but the most up-to-date listing for publications and their department heads is to be found in *PIMS* or *PR Planner*. The *UK Press Gazette* and *Media Week* will keep you up-to-date on appointment changes and new publications on the scene.

Using media abroad

Remember the overseas media. Some foreign publications will have a representative in the UK, but for others you may have to compile a personal mailing list. When you're dealing with news stories, remember the time differences. That goes, too, for telephone invitations – no one wants to be woken up in the middle of the night or at the crack of dawn to talk to a PR.

Radio

Don't dismiss radio, especially the local variety. The radio is portable and can offer more immediate returns. It is listened to at work, in the car, on holiday, at night.

TV and film

Television time is excellent when you can acquire it, but it can be very costly in man hours to fulfill your aim and you may be better off spreading the word by other methods. Try to think laterally about TV. If an airline is your client, you could offer stock library film to be used as backdrop for a TV film or series. If a product is immediately recognisable, it may be worthwhile to offer it as a giveaway on a game show. There can also be a PR aspect to feeding in information to Teletext. On the subject of electronic media, keep tabs on Internet.

Producing a video for mail-out or presentation purposes is also a costly procedure. Careful attention should be paid to budget before making this suggestion.

GETTING TO KNOW A PRODUCT

It behoves you to learn as much as you can about the product you are promoting. This is undoubtedly easier in-house as references are at your fingertips and the right people on the spot. Don't be afraid to ask questions – you do need to know from the sales force and technical division why the product in question is better than a competitor's.

Agency personnel are usually taken/sent on familiarisation trips to the factory/destination/hotel to get a feel for themselves of the advantages, and the downsides if there are any. As an objective eye, you may well want to offer constructive criticism on how a product might be improved or what is the best direction to take to promote it.

DEALING WITH PICTURES

They have been saying it for years:

> A picture is worth a thousand words . . . but only if the picture is right.

Study your publications and you will see the type of pictures they use. When you organise your own photo shoot, follow those clues.

Making a picture interesting

Some newspapers and magazines run product sections, in which case a straightforward shot of a product is exactly what's preferred. When it comes to hotel guest rooms or restaurants, the addition of people and action gives the picture a boost. The trades like an element of fun, too. A bunch of sales people wearing t-shirts logoed with a holiday company's name is better photographed in a situation rather than in a row. Movement in pictures – the tea-picker seen picking the tea as opposed to merely smiling to camera – also adds verve.

- All pictures should be captioned.

- The situation should be explained.

- Names should be named where appropriate.

- The address for return should be given.

Photo stocks

Not so long ago, keeping **photo stock (library)** would have come high on a PR's list, especially if the client were in the catering or travel industry. The advent of the CD Rom is beginning to change this, as destinations and agencies can send a sheet of available pictures via CD Rom for a publication to view (via computer) before selection. This doesn't mean the demise of the photo library, merely a change in format.

Having said that, there are still numerous smallish publications (especially those using freelance contributors who may not have such up-to-date computers) which ask for colour trannies. When they ask, and a PR complies in time, nine times out of ten those trannies are published, making the exercise most worthwhile.

CD Roms

Commenting on CD Roms, photographer Colin Anthill (see Case Study) says: 'At present the Rom acts as a shop window so the media can see which picture they want to use. Because so many images are crammed onto a CD, it takes a long time to download and is costly to produce the image selected into acceptable format. At present, that means when the image has been chosen, the picture 'bank' dupes the original tranny and sends it out. That's what I do myself. Eventually, the whole process will be handled by computers . . . but not just yet.'

CASE STUDY

Colin shares his expertise in photography

Colin Anthill took his first travel photograph back in 1959. Since 1962 he has run his own business and specialises in photography for the travel trade. He is so well known that companies frequently request him personally to cover their event, rather than one of his staff.

According to him, few PRs understand photography sufficiently to make it work for them. He explains: 'They call me up to ask for dupes of trannies when what they actually have in their hands are negatives – they don't seem to understand the difference. They will also attach a print to a note or comp slip by way of a paper clip which dents the photograph . . . irremovable when that photo is copied. It's not that PRs should know how to take photographs, merely be aware of some of the practicalities.

'When it comes to organising photo shoots for trade publications, some PRs think they know best, when in fact they have little understanding of what the publication is likely to use. As an example, let's say the client, an airline perhaps, might spend hundreds of pounds to have a thirty-foot long promotional banner made and the PR wants to put the airline's execs in a line behind it for a photo. This could be OK for in-house material, like the airline's own newsletter, but a publication like *Travel Trade Gazette* (TTG) would merely crop the banner out.'

Colin advises: 'Small logos are better, sited to show between the heads of the people and over their shoulders so they can't be cropped out. PRs don't seem to realise that every square inch of picture is revenue, so make sure faces are photographed close together. If the message is a new brochure, you don't want more than two faces shown with it. A line of ten people with a normal-sized brochure will merely mean the latter gets lost.

'Since paper went to four-colour, colour pictures are of prime importance and fetch awareness. If you're going to use props, make sure they're easily recognisable and not too big. Say a travel company wants to get across the message 'Don't take a gamble on holidays', all you need is the company's MD holding a pair of reasonably sized dice in his hands.

'If you're aiming for a page-one picture, keep it simple and instantly recognisable. The more complicated the picture, the less chance of it being published. Say you were organising a front-page picture for a Caribbean destination, then the sea, palm trees and perhaps one face sums it up.

'Banners and posters don't work between people. If you must show several executives, stand them in front and have them raise that poster or banner just a little so their heads and shoulders cut into it.

'It is impossible to make a conference speaker photo interesting. Most of these end up on the publication's cutting room floor, though sometimes if the caption gives the key phrase as it's being said the photo is 'live'.

'PRs should be as aware of deadlines for pictures as much as for copy. Take a prize draw at an ABTA conference or World Travel Market exhibition. The last (TTG) conference edition comes out on Thursday, yet the prize draw is happening on Wednesday night. If the picture is taken Wednesday night it will miss the deadline. So fake the shot one day early, editorial can whack in the winner's name at the last minute. The same is true at the start of an event. One tourist board wanted me to wait until the first day of the show because its stand wasn't completed. I pointed out that I wanted a tight corner shot and the corner was fine. What's more, the exec's jeans wouldn't be seen because it was a closeup. Result? Picture made the first TTG edition in the morning.'

Colin's photo opportunity advice can be summed up as:

● Give a publication the type of picture it usually uses.

● Make pictures interesting.

● Go for colour.

● Don't include too many people.

● Opt for closeups.

● Take care with banners/poster/brochures.

● Fake a 'live' shot early to make the press.

● Keep a picture uncomplicated.

● Know the difference between a negative and transparency.

SUMMARY

The following rules will help you acquire basic knowledge:

- learn and practise writing skills

- study what makes a good picture

- respond effectively to press enquiries

- understand how the media works.

5
Understanding Media Relations

Supplying literature, pictures and entertainment is part and parcel of any PR's work, wherever they're based and whoever their clients. Preparing for special events is also part of a PR's working day, much of it spent arranging for paperwork or on the telephone. For an event, there are three major aspects:

- press kit
- photographs
- event programme (launch).

PUTTING TOGETHER A PRESS KIT

It is standard procedure to send or hand out press kits before or during a product launch or briefing. As its name suggests, a kit is a pack of information useful to a journalist, but the amount of material necessary for inclusion will depend upon the product. The launch of a new ship, for example, could result in a very fat pack containing the following:

- news release
- technical information
- design
- personnel profiles
- backgrounder
- cruise brochure
- photograph(s).

Press kits have their own company-logoed folders and should include a business card of the PR involved.

Giving a gift

Sometimes a client will want a press gift given out with the press kit, as a thank you for attending, but also to act as a reminder of the occasion/event.

It goes without saying that budget will restrict the type of gift, but when you can influence the client to make it 'different' and useful, so much the better. There are thousands of journalists with office drawerfuls of logoed key rings.

Gifts

Do you give clients gifts at Christmas? This is a question only you can answer. No, it's not compulsory, but if the gifts in question are well thought out, this may be a worthwhile gesture. A personally signed copy of a book; a bottle of very good champagne; a no-strings lunch or dinner invitation . . . these could all work in your favour. Please note, no gifts are intended as bribes, only as sweeteners. In some ways, this type of utilisation of PR may be considered old-fashioned, but providing it is not overdone it can help cement media relations.

SUPERVISING A PHOTO SHOOT

It is generally left up to the PR to arrange for a photographer to cover a press event, but the photographer will need to be briefed and should be accompanied. Specialised areas such as food or jewellery will be shot in a studio and require a specialist photographer. At a press conference, however, it may be a simple matter of shots of key speakers.

Decide on which type of publications you want to target with the photograph and style it accordingly (see Dealing with Pictures Chapter 4).

Although not imperative, when you accompany a press group on a facility trip, it is a nice gesture to take informal photographs of the invitees and send each of them one after the trip is over.

The photo call

When you feel you can take advantage of a photo opportunity, appraise the press with the news prior to the event. In this case, you are inviting press photographers to take their own pictures, although you'd be well advised to have a cameraman of your own present as well. Events like the unveiling of a new car, or visit by an overseas celebrity, are the type to warrant the photo call route.

GIVING A PRESS LAUNCH

The three main ways of giving a launch are:

- conference
- lunch
- cocktail party.

All three require meticulous planning, invitations, refreshment, costing in (or over) your fee. Try to ensure that:

- your event does not clash with another

- a venue is suitable and easily accessible

- timing appeals to the type of media you hope will attend.

Arranging a press conference

An invitation to attend a press conference need only be as simple as one sheet of letter-headed paper or fax. Short notice is also acceptable and expected hospitality minimal: a coffee preceding the briefing, a drink afterwards.

Conferences are held regularly for parliamentary and financial press, but in other instances they are held because something unexpected has occurred, or because a visiting VIP has asked a PR to organise one.

If you are referring to the event as 'a conference', make sure something newsworthy is going to be said. Professional journalists don't want to waste their time. If it's merely a case of Mr B's in town, come and meet him, or Company C is launching its umpteenth brochure, which hasn't really changed much, make the invitation a 'reception' or more casual meeting.

Timing
Because a PR is frequently asked to organise a press conference at short notice, it may not always be possible to time it

appropriately. If you have some control, two key factors to consider are:

- press deadlines
- morning appeals.

Venue
Any venue that is used as a conference or briefing session is fine, providing enough seating is available and there are microphones. When a video screening is to be given, make sure you know how the machine works (if being held in a hotel) or can readily lay hands on technical support services.

Arranging a press lunch
This could actually be breakfast or dinner, as much as a lunch, and is a good event for informal discussion prior to or after a presentation. When you target-market media, smaller numbers are more rewarding, even if you have to give more than one lunch over a period of days. It is also best to seat press by place names. If the occasion is a hotel opening, and there is a greater blanket invitation, a buffet meal should suffice and place name seating be unnecessary. If the event is a sit-down meal given as a thank you, you may want to use the words 'By invitation only' and request specified, named journalists.

The meal time presentation
Invariably, except perhaps for the thank you situation, there is a **presentation**. It may be a welcome address, a speech with question time to follow, or a video. Whichever it is, and it could be all three, there are some dos and don'ts:

- Keep speeches short.

- Keep question time to a minimum.

- Videos should not be longer than fifteen minutes.

- Presentations are best before meals.

Timing

These days, many busy journalists prefer breakfast briefings/
presentations, but bear in mind that some of your guests will
not live round the corner, so make allowances for transportation
timing. If it is a lunch, give a '12.30 for 1 pm' style of invitation.
While you may not be able to stick rigidly to your schedule, try
not to let timing get out of hand, even if you are still waiting
for that VIP media person who hasn't yet turned up.

Venue

Your selection will depend upon budget, reason for the event
and numbers, but good catering and service is essential whether
you are planning a buffet or sit-down affair. If the selected venue
is a hotel or restaurant, be sure to warn staff in advance about
any speech/question time that is being featured before the meal,
so they can plan their service accordingly.

Arranging a press reception

Generally, a press reception is a cocktail party and involves
large numbers of guests. Journalists are less likely to confirm
their attendance for this type of party so it takes experienced
assessment to guestimate final numbers . . . and there are always
no-shows even if they have said yes at the time. Press guests will
expect some kind of speech, and/or slide or video presentation,
but keep them short and time them for around the middle of
allocated reception time.

Timing

More than likely a reception takes place after work. Be sure to
stipulate the duration, but be prepared for it to run over by at
least a half-hour. Some of those journalists who do attend
cocktail parties will stay on for as long as the booze flows, so
there should be a final cut-off time for the bar.

Remembering follow-up

It is sad but true that many of your invited guests will not let
you know whether or not they are attending the function to
which you have invited them. In the case of the sit-down meal
especially, this could cost a client wasted money, so make sure
you follow up acceptances with a confirmatory call and ask

those who have not responded whether or not they are coming. In the past, this would have seemed like nagging, now it is simply a matter of using good commercial sense.

Issuing invitations
Invitations to any event may be made by letter, fax, phone or printed card. If the product is particularly glamorous, or the event especially grand, the invitation should match up in appearance.

An innovative invitation is more likely to be remembered and answered than the run-of-the-mill one because it stands out of what inevitably will be a pile.

ARRANGING A PRESS TRIP

This can be the most harrowing planned experience of all. If the press trip is a day's visit to a factory/stately home/city or specific attraction, the arrangements will be easier than if it involves travel abroad for a few days or more.

You must start with a timed programme even if subsequent changes will be made. For a facility trip in this country or outside, you will need to give:

- pick-up point and return information

- contact phone numbers

- some reasonable idea of itinerary.

Going abroad
When the press trip is headed overseas, the ideal pre-planning is to have done the itinerary yourself first, as a kind of rehearsal.

You will want to invite the type of media considered most useful to your client/company, but if you are working with others (airlines, hotels, tourist boards, etc), you may have to accept some press invitees of their choice. Overseas facility trips are designed to raise the profile of a destination, or calm fears about it, or to show something new. The trip should never be too long and the itinerary should always be interesting, though not so jam-packed that guests can't catch their breath.

Accountancy
Adult & further education
Advertising
Advertising & media law
Aerospace
African trade
Agricultural engineering
Agricultural science journals
Agricultural journals overseas
Aircraft engineering
Airports & airlines
Ambulance services
Amusement business
Anaesthesia
Arable farming
Archaeology
Architecture
Architecture & preservation
Army
Article numbering
Arts & craft teaching
Association management
Audio visual
Automation
Aviation
Baking trade
Banking
Bee-keeping
Brewing trade
Broadcast & film
Building
Building materials
Building society
Business
Business equipment
Business magazines
Business training
Business travel
Business women
Camping & caravanning
Caribbean trade
Catering trade

Cattle
Ceramics
Character licensing &
  merchandising
Charity management
Chemicals
Chemistry
Chemists & pharmaceuticals
Child education
Children's wear
Chiropody
Cleaning & maintenance
Club management
Coach & bus
Coal industry
Commercial & industrial law
Commodities
Company secretary
Computer design
Computer education
Computer user magazines
Computing
Concrete
Confectionary trade
Confectioners, tobacconists,
  newsagents
Copyright & patent law
Corrosion
Cosmetic trade
Craft trade
Credit & HP
Criminal law
Dairy farming
Dairy trade
Defence
Demolition
Dentistry
Design
Diplomacy
Drama & dance teaching
Drinks trade
Economics

Fig. 5. Specialised media listed in *PIMS*' trade and
technical section.

Education
Educational equipment
Electrical engineering
Electrical power
Electrical trade
Electricity
Electronic engineering & design
Electronics trade
Energy & power
Engineering
Engineering design
English language teaching
Environment
European business
Exhibitions & conferences
Export
Family law
Farming
Fashion trade
Feedstuffs
Ferrous and non-ferrous metals
Finance
Finishing
Fire service
Fishing trade
Fleet & company cars
Flooring
Floristry
Food manufacturing
Footwear & leather
Forestry
Frozen foods trade
Fruit trade
Funeral services
Furnishing
Garden trade
Gas industry
General practitioners
Geographical & geological
Geography teaching
Geriatric medicine
Gift trade
Glass trade
Goats
Graphics
Grocery trade

Hairdressing & beauty trade
Hardware
Health food trade
Health retailing
Healthcare trade
Heating & air conditioning
History teaching
Home teaching
Horticulture
Hospital construction
Hospital doctors
Hospitals
Hotel trade
Housing
Hygiene
Industrial equipment
Industrial relations
Industry
Information processing
Insulation
Insurance
Interior design
Investment
Jewellery & horology
Judicial law
Kitchens, bedrooms, bathrooms
Knitting & hosiery
Laboratory equipment
Landscape architecture
Languages
Latin American trade
Laundry
Law
Libraries
Licensed trade
Livestock
Local government
Lubrication
Management & administration
Market traders
Marketing
Materials handling & storage
Mathematics
Meat trade
Mechanical engineering
Medical journals

Medical laboratory
Medical miscellaneous
Men's wear
Metals
Metalworking & machine tools
Meteorology
Middle East trade
Mining & quarrying
Motor accessories
Motor traders
Motor transport
Motorcycle & bicycle trade
Motoring school
Music trade
Navy
Non-destructive testing
Nuclear power
Nursing & midwifery
Obstetrics & gynaecology
Occupational health
Oil & petroleum
Opthalmology
Optics
Overseas hospitals
Overseas trade
Packaging & bottling
Painting & decorating
Paints, pigments, resins
Paper trade
Parks & sports grounds
Pensions
Personnel
Pet trade
Photographic trade
Picture framing
Pig farming
Planning
Plant hire & equipment
Plant science
Plastics, rubbers & polymers
Plumbing
Police
Post-graduate medicine
Poultry
Power
Pre-school & playgroup

Press & media
Printing
Process engineering
Property law
Property trade
Protection
Public law
Public relations
Publishing
Purchasing
Radiology
Railways
Reading
Refrigeration
Religious education
Retailing & merchandising
Road construction
Roofing
Safety
Security
Sales
Science
Science teaching
Sea transport
Secretarial
Security retailing
Sewing machines
Sheep farming
Show biz
Small business
Social science
Social service & welfare
Software
Special education
Speech therapy
Sponsorship
Sports & leisure
Sports & physical education
Standards & measures
Stationery
Stone industries
Supermarkets
Surgery
Surveying
Tax & duty free
Taxation

Taxation law	Venture capital
Taxi trade	Veterinary
Teaching	Video trade
Telecommunications	Waste management
Textiles	Water service
Tobacco trade	Window trade
Toy trade	Women's wear
Trades unions	Woodworking & timber
Training magazines	Word processing
Transport & freight	Work study
Travel trade	Works & maintenance
Tunnelling	Zoology
Vending	

LOOKING AT SPECIALISED MEDIA

For many PRs, 'niche market' (specialised) media is of priority importance. It exists for almost every subject, as you can see in the example in Figure 5. As you can see from all the list, there are plenty of markets to tap for a variety of products/services for which you may be doing PR. Many specialised publications prove useful vehicles for raising the profile of a person or organisation.

Profile raising
Targeting particular publications can be used to get a person and/or organisation better known and associated with a set of ideas. If this is your quest, the two first questions to ask are:

● Who do you want to reach?
● What do you want to say?

CASE STUDY

Francis tackles profile raising
Francis Beckett is a published author who teaches journalism studies part-time and has worked on profile raising PR projects over the years.

'One project was for the General Common and Municipal

Boiler Makers trade union (GMB), whose aim was to recruit people working in local government and woo them away from a rival and leading trade union. In this case, the target market was everyone who worked in local government. The client's message was: We are interested in the issues that concern you. Our job was to ensure our client was associated in the target market's minds with those issues concerning them, such as compulsory competitive tenders, a scheme which meant a lot of them lost their jobs due to privatisation.

'How to reach our target market? There were only two truly appropriate publications: *Local Government Journal* and *Municipal Journal*. We needed our client's name constantly appearing in those publications. If a PR can come up with a reasonable news story that embraces quotes on subjects of concern, and knows the publication deadlines, that job gets done. The magazines might even let us write a feature for them. When this is professionally done, the publication is happy – it's free to them – and we're happy because we're raising profile. Sometimes these articles might appear under the client's name, which is even better for raising profile.'

The mission in this instance was accomplished and membership increased. Francis points out: 'You target those publications which are likely to be read by those you want to reach. For instance, right now I put together a magazine for the Masters of Business Administration (MBAs) and am besieged by head hunters who are offering me regular columns for free because their target audience is my readership. If they wanted straightforward advertising, they could pay for it, but they're looking for below-the-line coverage. One head hunter is therefore writing an article for me on how to write a CV. His only pay back is the line at the end that says Mr A is managing director of Z agency.'

SUMMARY

Understanding the media requires you to:

• be an excellent arranger

• take advantage of specialised publications.

6
Being a Spokesperson

Any official PR is considered a spokesperson, able and allowed to air approved views to both press and public, whether they work for a company, agency or a particular individual. However, one person may be particularly responsible as 'the mouthpiece'.

SPEAKING ON BEHALF OF OTHERS

The company spokesperson
This is a position of responsibility, demanding the kind of experience that can deal with an unexpected or catastrophic situation at the drop of a hat.

Although the spokesperson could well have a personal or telephone briefing before projecting a company line, he or she has to be so imbued with company policy and workings that they know, without being told, the type of message to be relayed for any contingency.

> **Many high-profile companies designate a particular PR person to be the official mouthpiece, to whom the regular PR or press department staff will have to refer before making official comment.**

When Lord Charles Forte, for example, owned the Forte brand of hotels, there was a PR department for each of the company's divisions as well as a spokesman for Lord Charles himself. The same is true for Virgin Atlantic. In addition to a press office for the airline, and another for Virgin Holidays, assisting outside agencies for the hotel side and other product divisions, a specific Virgin spokesperson is given the job of speaking on behalf of Richard Branson.

If a bomb goes off in a hotel, or an airliner crashes, very often it is the PR who is the first port of call for the media, and who must therefore act as the company's initial shield. There may not be time to reach the CEO, or the latter may not be readily accessible to either the media or their own PR. In such a situation, the PR is on their own to handle things as deftly, and as quickly, as possible.

Speaking on behalf of a celebrity

Similarly, the publicist must know the client so well that answers to simple questions can roll off their tongue as smoothly as if the client themselves were doing the answering.

The agency spokesperson

Because of the intimate nature, a designated spokesperson is more likely to be employed by a company itself than a PR agency. When PR agency personnel are spokespeople, their brief is more likely to be concerned with reporting comment, say on behalf of a merger or a new architectural project.

The following are among the most likely to need a spokesperson:

- hotel groups
- airlines
- shipping companies
- government
- large public companies.

What attributes are necessary?

Good spokespeople should possess the following talents:

- eloquence
- experience
- company knowledge
- quick assessment of facts
- speedy action
- excellent judgment.

CRISIS MANAGEMENT

Crisis management is the most difficult situation for a spokesperson. Here we are not talking about making mountains out of molehills, or stirring storms in teacups, but handling a volatile situation which could erupt into a crisis, or a crisis which has already taken place.

Take an outbreak of food poisoning or disease in such a public domain as a hotel, plane or ship. If news of it can be contained or curtailed, so much the better, but expert judgment is essential if fingers don't want to be burned. When the public domain itself is newsworthy, it might be better to suffer the onslaught of bad publicity over a short period of time, and let it die down naturally, than disregard it altogether.

Before the age of electronic media, covering up unwanted exposure was much easier. Nowadays, lying only makes things worse. Like terriers, the media hang on to every grain of truth they can, ever ready to make it a headline. If there are rules to try to adhere to, they are:

- evade not avoid
- speech not silence.

The phrase 'no comment' is a very detrimental one. It only confirms what is unsaid. Making a statement can give the facts, whitewash the facts, change focus of facts, but is always reported.

The PR's job is to find out all the facts as quickly as possible, let the media know what those facts are and what is being done to resolve an undesired situation.

In some cases, it may be best to put out a statement with answers to questions which have yet to be asked.

There are so many possible hazards that it is best to cover the possibility of them occurring in advance. The PR who is prepared for the unlikely can swing into action a great deal more quickly than the PR who has refused to contemplate misfortune.

The two necessities are:

- be prepared
- be realistic.

Keeping control

The skilled PR manager will be able to satisfy the media yet still keep control. Even when a question cannot be answered, for whatever reason, the PR should explain why an answer is not possible.

Always:

- Report your own bad news: better from you than another source.

- Provide back-up evidence to statements.

- Keep a record of any events during a crisis.

- Be frank but don't exaggerate a situation.

- Stick to agreed policy procedures.

Capable handling of a difficult situation can result in a better image for the company, better communication with the media and more recognition of the PR function by key management. For some industries, normally hazardous situations may even achieve public acceptance.

Training to cope with a crisis

It may be necessary to ensure that other personnel within a company are trained to prepare for a potential disaster. Telephonists and/or receptionists may have to deal with calls regarding the dead or injured. There may be legal aspects which have to be considered. In crisis management, there is an anticipated situation whereby switchboard operators and top management must be aware and trained for eventualities. Some companies may even have a crisis committee which meets regularly whether or not a crisis has yet occurred.

The key phrases are:

- What if?
- What to do?

Bad news is good news

What is bad news for a PR is all too frequently good news for the media. When disaster strikes, a PR must be ready to follow up an initial statement with more detailed ones and offer the media facilities so they can best report the situation accurately. Once a problem has been resolved, the same media should be contacted and told or shown what has been done/why the problem no longer exists.

Product recall

Justified bad publicity may result in product recall, such as the instance when glass was found in a jar of baby food, or when it was discovered how easily the Baby Benz car overturns. Occasionally, it may behove a company to advertise the recall rather than rely on press pickup alone.

Product recall following bad publicity might ultimately result in good publicity. A faulty product, for example, can be relaunched as a vastly improved one.

DON'T BREATHE A WORD

So when should a PR keep mum? Even in court, where a witness is required to swear to 'the truth, the whole truth and nothing but the truth', what is said can be edited. A party guilty of manslaughter, killing someone who broke into their home, naturally opts for a self defence charge, not premeditated murder, even though at the time they might have tried to kill the intruder.

> **It takes finely tuned judgment to know when to give and when to omit information.**

On occasions a PR is hired specifically to keep things out of the press. Most celebrities, for example, are publicity seekers, but there are times when, for personal or security reasons, they wish to remain anonymous. Hotel PRs frequently have to deny certain guests are staying under their roof; Buckingham Palace's press office often refutes rumours and gossip, even when there is some truth to them.

As time goes by
The public's memory is short so it is pointless to hark back to a disaster which happened some time ago, unless forced to. Only remind people if the solution to a problem is a much improved product.

KNOWING WHAT'S NEWS

Some news is obvious, when it is of interest either to the general public at large, or to a specific audience, such as a medical breakthrough. For some PRs 'news' is a far greyer area, to be found only by sifting through the information given them and adapting it into a sensible news story.

Examples of newsworthy items might include:

- Surgeon performs first heart transplant in the UK.

- Businessman creates 'no frills' airline.

- Major tour operation goes bust.

- High street fashion chain sold to the Saudis.

All the above are obvious news stories which the media will wish to report.

Examples of when a PR must be creative to find news might include:

- New refurbishment for London hotel.

- Jug kettle replaces the traditional.

- New menu for restaurant.

Creating news

Let's look at how a PR might treat the above in order to spark
press interest.

Refurbishment

Questions to ask client or company before giving this out as
news could comprise:

● Has new technology been installed?

● Did the overhaul include miles of wiring/gold leafing/carpet,
etc?

● How has refurbishment responded to customer demand?

● Is there 'a first'?

Jug kettle replacement

● Why has the traditional kettle disappeared?

● What are a jug kettle's benefits?

● Is it helpful to the environment, cuts down on wastage?

● Has kitchen design changed?

New menu

● Does an increased number of vegetarians warrant new
menu?

● Has red meat given way to fish predominance?

● Do smaller appetites call for smaller portions, smaller price?

Once you can answer such questions, it should be possible to
turn a 'blah' release into interesting and positive news.

SELLING A FEATURE IDEA

The PR with creative thought does have the opportunity to suggest a topic for an article or programme that will encompass a client.

A hypothetical case

A PR whose client is a 50+ dress designer who is having to compete fiercely with younger, more trendy designers making the magazine fashion pages. The PR suggests to a Sunday supplement features editor that a piece on 50+ ladies with a size 10 figure could go down well, the client being one of them. The idea is accepted, raising profile and giving coverage to the client, wearing her own design. The idea is accepted, but the editor wants to use the PR herself in the feature. This too is good, raising profile of the PR company in question.

A second hypothetical situation . . .

The PR's client manufactures aromatherapy oils. The PR suggests to a women's magazine beauty editor that they run a piece on the A–Z of aromatherapy. It will include the client as one of the spokespeople explaining what aromatherapy is all about, what it can do for the average woman and how it can be used in the home.

. . . and a third

The PR's client is an insurance company. The PR suggests the editor of the money pages of a newspaper consider a piece on rip-offs, including the client's advice on what questions to ask a potential insurance company, what pitfalls to look out for, how to assess a good policy. The idea is accepted; the client is shown in a positive light on the plus side of the business.

SITTING IN ON INTERVIEWS

When an arranged client interview might be a sticky one, it is often a good idea for the PR to sit in. Should there be language difficulties, this becomes an essential to act as translator. And if the client is not a good talker or responsive interviewee, the PR can help matters along with prompter phrases or remarks.

The client who lacks media confidence or is unsure of what will be asked, requests a PR's presence more for assurance than anything else. The professional PR, however, will have the knack of steering the interviewer away from undesired subjects and onto the planned publicity course, without making hackles rise or voicing too many unwanted interruptions.

Training for interviews

It may be necessary for a client/company executive to be trained for media interviews so that they may come across in the best way. This is especially true for television. Several organisations specialise in interview techniques and it may be worth a PR sending a client for a day's session.

Before a press conference, briefing or presentation, it is part of the PR's job to anticipate questions from the media which may arise and discuss these with the client in advance. Possible answers to such hypothetical questions can then also be suggested.

CASE STUDIES

PR copes with a shipping fiasco . . .

The 1994 refit of the QE2 was something of a fiasco, since this major refurbishment programme was not finished by the time of the first cruise. It was such a good story for the tabloids, there was no way of keeping it out of print or out of hand. Regular statements were therefore issued, informing what was happening and PR did their best to answer all queries.

Realising that passengers on board would have access to local news and phone, for a personal story, the only sensible way of dealing with potential disastrous publicity was to offer passengers a compensatory package before they demanded it. This was the advice put on paper to the company, and subsequently accepted.

. . . and with a potential crisis

When a small case of food poisoning on board the ship threatened to become a major story, speedy action by the PR prevented it. By getting in touch with the medical people and assessing every case of sickness, all of which are recorded, it was possible to build up a true picture of what was happening. Issuing a statement too fast, of course, could go wrong, but in the case of a major outbreak it is best to inform people as factually as possible as to what is happening, and being done, so the situation can be put into proper context.

A PR overlooks backfire

In the 1980s AIDS was a key topic. However, when one cruise ship passenger subsequently died after disembarking at one of the ports of call, the PR's advice was to say nothing, considering the case simply a personal tragedy. However, events overtook. The local paper at the port of call got hold of the story and panic broke out. A statement had to be issued. Deciding when to keep quiet is never easy. Sometimes it can backfire.

SUMMARY

If you are a spokesperson, be prepared for the following:

* being in the firing line

* having to train others

* knowing interview techniques thoroughly

* having absolute authority.

7
Working as a Freelancer

When you work as a freelancer you are running your own business. Although it is possible to wear a PR hat part time, say for one account, and do something else for the rest of your work week, the outcome is generally not very satisfactory. Therefore, it becomes a question of balancing your outgoing costings with your incoming fees, to your financial advantage.

Most people choosing the freelance option have earned their skills and gained experience elsewhere first. Reasons why they select to go freelance can be many and varied, from raising a family to the prospect of better finances.

The freelance PR will operate in the same way as the agency or in-house counterpart, but will need more self-discipline to make things work for them.

ASSESSING THE PLUS FACTORS

Although the freelance PR could well rent a separate office, one of the biggest plus factors is that you can work out of home and can control your own time if you wish. Undoubtedly, you will need to get out and about some of the time, but you won't have the daily hassle of depending upon public transport to reach an office, or leave it, at a specific hour.

Having direct contact

When you are heading up your own business, you are likely to contract with and report to the head of the client company, which cuts corners when attempting to attain information and/or quotes. Unlike perhaps the account executive or manager in an outside agency, you are put through directly to the head of a company.

In addition to the benefits to you, this enables you to offer that extra something to the client company concerned. They know they are getting your personal attention; you know they have your trust. Despite the fact that you should manage your own time effectively to allow for weekends and holidays, getting hold of you is more possible than if you worked somewhere else. The thought that you are available at all times is of great reassurance to many potential companies.

Having more control

When you control your own business, you not only have control of office time structure but also when and if you wish to quit an account. Whilst in an agency you may be stuck with an account you do not particularly relish, the freelance has no need to accept or dismiss an account.

As a business header, you control funds. You can ask yourself about the necessity of a new computer, second or third phone line, more assistants, etc.

> As a freelancer you offer truly personalised attention, which is something agency personnel can rarely do, and for a lower cost in most cases.

Also, you can choose which accounts to pitch for, those in which you are most interested or know the most about. They, in turn, are buying your talents, skills and expertise in their given field more cost effectively than if they paid a large, well known, named agency.

As a freelancer your work may well be varied, so you enjoy similar benefits to those of an agency: different press relations, different day-to-day work structure, diverse activities.

Summing up the plus factors

- You can opt to work at home.

- You liaise directly with company chiefs.

- You have control of your time.

- You can pick your own accounts.

- You are personally involved at all times.

- Your day is as varied as that in an agency.

WATCHING OUT FOR THE PITFALLS

Working for and by yourself can be a lonely occupation. With no counterpart staff to discuss problems or ask questions of, you do run the risk that the in-house PR runs: lack of objectivity or seeing with a clear eye.

> **If you are the one setting your schedule, more discipline is needed than in the average work situation.**

If you cannot keep to your own time management, you could have big problems. If you are working at home, the temptation is to take time out to do the washing/play with the kids/have coffee with friends at times which are not beneficial to you.

Dealing with detail

To go it alone for the first time can be difficult. You may have been used to medical, pension, insurance benefits; now you must deal with them for yourself. You may have been used to ordering stationery/ribbons/tapes without a thought for their cost; now you must make a note of every financial outgoing. You may not have thought twice about that international phone call; now you need to log costs so you know exactly what you are spending. And unless you have built it into your fee, entertainment expenses must be more carefully considered.

Taking on too much

One of the biggest pitfalls is greed. You take on too many accounts whose needs you simply can't fulfill. This means you either hire more staff or run yourself ragged, maybe losing some of those accounts in the interim. Remember, you cannot be in two places at once so time management is of ultimate importance. Like the agency account manager, you must know how much time to allocate to each account each week, even if your hours are more flexible.

Remember, too, you'll have to pitch for an account yourself, with no support help from staff. Writing a proposal is a time consuming effort for which you may not have the resources.

Structuring fees

While an agency knows the overhead costs it must cover to earn a profit, and will accordingly only work for the right fees, for the freelancer this area can be a nightmare. When you are self-employed it is very hard to say no to work, even if the fee offered is low. Charge too much and you may lose a job; charge too little and you lose credibility.

If you have no assistants, an accountant will probably advise you to opt for a retainer fee that is exclusive of print and mailing costs, whenever you can. Dealing with print work can be a very sticky business unless you know precisely what you are doing. Generally, the cost of an event is a separate expense paid by a client, but one-to-one entertaining may be down to you.

Summing up the pitfalls

- Working by yourself can be lonely.

- To work at home requires great discipline.

- There are no company benefits.

- Office equipment must be purchased.

- Previous experience is recommended.

- Pitching for an account may prove more difficult.

SETTING UP AN OFFICE

If you are setting up an office from scratch, you will need some capital. To work from home this might be achieved with a couple of hundred pounds; to work outside, a couple of thousand. Wherever it might be, there are three absolute necessities for an office:

- telephone
- equipment
- stationery.

Setting up at home

Even those freelance PRs who eventually rent office space elsewhere generally start off working at home, where one room should be set aside specifically for work purposes.

Two telephone lines are a necessity, one for personal calls, one for business ones. This will help keep accounts straight at the end of the financial year.

You don't need whizz bang equipment. After all, you are not trying to be a Satchi & Satchi, but you do need a computer, an answer machine, fax machine and photocopier.

Stationery supplies are essential, and that includes headed paper, comp slips and business cards. Make sure you know or learn something about print costs.

Another must: keep strict note of all your business expenses. This is not only to ensure your fee is working profitably for you, but is necessary for tax returns. Most freelancers consider hiring an accountant essential.

Summing up the advantages of working from home

- No real overheads:

- Always available.

- No wasted travel time.

Renting office space

If you are not going to work from home, hunt around for the most economical office space. It may behove you to merely rent a desk in someone else's office to begin with rather than take on a whole room to yourself.

Many complexes of small offices rented by self-employed people have a general switchboard which will take messages.

This is to your advantage and saves the bother of an answer machine. When you share an office you are able to enjoy some camaraderie and may well have someone to man the fort if you have to go out unexpectedly.

Be aware that your rental and service costs are likely to be payable before your fee money is paid, so you do need some capital before you start.

Incomings per month		Outgoings per month	
A/C A Fee	£_____	Office rent	£_____
A/C B Fee	£_____	Service charge	£_____
A/C C Fee	£_____	Telephone	£_____
		Any equipment hire	£_____
TOTAL	£_____	Stationery	£_____
		Insurance	£_____
		Pension plan	£_____
		Contingencies	£_____
		Transport	£_____
		TOTAL	£_____

Fig. 6. Assessing the finances of setting up an office.

Do try to be sure that rental costs are worth it. Write yourself a list of incomings and outgoings like the one in Figure 6. If the net sum between the two sets of figures shows a reasonable profit, it may be worth renting outside. Your contingency figure, however, needs to cover situations like late payment by the client and/or loss of an account.

Summing up the advantages of renting office space

- general switchboard
- support services
- camaraderie.

MANAGING TIME

Ask any freelance PR what they dislike most about work in an agency, and they will tell you 'interminable meetings'. In fact, wherever you are based, you could spent the majority of your day in meetings and get very little practical work done. Equally, you could spend the majority of your time entertaining, achieving little more of a result than if you more effectively used that time on the phone.

Self-employed PRs say they spend sixty per cent of their day on the phone and forty per cent otherwise engaged. You need to be able to cost out your hours and what they're worth in pounds and pence, whether or not a cheque for their worth is on the table then and there. You must balance 'investment time' against 'priorities' and adjust your time input accordingly.

A number of management consultants conduct seminars on the very subject of time management. These could be worth paying for and attending.

One thing the lecturers will tell you to do is write down a list of your priorities, the 'must dos'. When a journalist's deadline is tomorrow, and you have the chance of press exposure, then fulfilling that journalist's requirements becomes a must do. If a client's report is needed on the MD's desk by 9 am, and this client is of financial importance, fulfilling the requirement becomes a must do.

Your check list includes:

- Don't get distracted.

- Write a list of priorities.

- Stick to a schedule.

CHANGING A CAREER

Don't think that just because you've spent several years in one career that you can't move into PR. Providing you read up, have a disciplined mind that is quick to learn, and an outgoing personality, the PR door is open.

The most likely move is from journalism into PR. The

advantage is a natural one: you know the press and what they need. A move from sales or marketing is another normal step; you may well have liaised with PR.

There is another likely move: from the City into financial PR. Many senior business people, such as analysts, have taken this route.

CASE STUDIES

Jacquie runs her own business from home

Jacquie Richardson has run her own business from home for the past twenty-five years. 'I was a failed actress so went to work for the BBC on the Arts side, then headed for a PR agency as a secretary where I was lucky enough to have an MD who encouraged me to get stuck in. I took the IPR exams to become a member. When I decided to go it alone, I sent postcards to everyone I knew, and some work came my way.

'When you work as a freelancer you work intensively but the client always gets *you* instead of being passed from one minnion to another as at an agency. I tend only to work with board directors or proprietors and therefore play an influential role. My clients do take my advice but they leave me to get on with things. I may not be their full-time employee, but I am an integral part of their strategies. What's more, there's no waste of time in endless meetings as frequently happens in agencies.

'You do have to be very disciplined and in fact have less free time than in other PR situations. You can't go and do the gardening in the middle of the day. I work between 8.30 am and 7.30 pm, but I do try to keep the rest of the evening and my weekends free, even though some journalists will call me at those times.

'It can be very lonely, but there is a wonderful network of other PRs. I do ninety per cent of my work over the phone, which certainly saves on transport costs, but this could make some people feel isolated.

'These days I have a purpose-built office at home. Home can be anywhere, clients don't visit me, I visit them when necessary. I do have a computer, two phone lines, fax machine, ansaphone and photocopier, but I don't really think a mobile phone is essential.

'The advantage of working at home is there are few overheads, which is how I survived the recession. But I think many people these days go freelance expecting to make a lot of money. A one-man band is not going to make £100,000 a year, the client with that budget is going to want an all-singing, all-dancing agency.

'Being self-employed means you never really know what you're going to earn in the course of a year. I religiously set aside money for tax because I know I could be left with no clients or a large tax bill at any given time.

'Client companies who choose an agency do so because they like the sexy image, like to refer to 'my agency' and be able to walk into smart, glamorous offices. They desire the power of monthly meetings. But they are paying for all that, which effectively can be a waste of money. On the downside, I don't have the resources to make huge elaborate presentations or proposals, and some companies would want those.

'Yes, it is difficult to work on an hourly rate and figure it out per day. Sometimes you can go wrong. Usually, though, there is some leeway for negotiation depending upon the type of client. Fees do vary. Computer people, for example, expect to pay more. A family-owned restaurant cannot afford to do so.

'Annual retainers are obviously the best loved contracts, but much work is on a project basis which is less satisfactory. The freelance PR must be very focused.

'I had thought of renting an office, but then people can reach me twenty-four hours a day here and I don't have to think about getting up to take the Northern Line. I prefer to spend the money on an assistant (which I now have) rather than on an office outside.

'I do now have an insurance policy to cover the contingency of not being able to work at all and anyone considering being self-employed should think hard about a pension plan.'

Jane rents space in a serviced office

Jane Herbert's background is in sales, particularly advertising sales for publishing companies. She moved into PR six years ago, operating her own company from home.

'Because I had to work closely with the editorial teams, my "selling" activities ended up as a PR role although when I first set up my own office it was in marketing communications. That meant I was offering a menu of services, of which PR was one item. Because I understood how magazines worked, and because I did a lot of reading and self-training, PR business came my way.'

After two years at home, Jane decided to branch out by renting a serviced office in her home area. 'Business had expanded and I needed support services, people to answer phones, type whatever was needed. In a business office complex, everyone pays for a share of those services which certainly saves going every time to Pronto Print.

'Freelance PRs who rent separate offices usually do so because of growth of business. With four ongoing clients and more in the offing, I felt I needed the extra space. The idea of a new account probably covers the rent.

'When you rent a serviced office you know what the costs are going to be . . . and I don't just mean rent. Also there is a possibility of a short let, say three months, at the end of which time you know whether you're going to land on your feet or fall over backward.

'As a freelance PR, I charge in advance so I don't think a shortfall is a problem. It's a safeguard before you take on work to know those fee payment terms. When business expands you need more space, something I simply didn't have at home. You wouldn't move unless the amount of business warranted it. Also it's an image thing, having someone answer the phone and take messages instead of leaving it to an answer machine.

'You might well take your own pc with you, but in a serviced office the most up-to-date equipment is available on a rental basis, like the latest colour copiers. If you don't have your own fax machine there is a general one, E-mail too.'

Jane has her own room plus use of meeting space and has since taken on a business partner and an assistant. 'As your business grows you can move into a bigger room, should it shrink, you can move into a smaller one. If you grow really big you may be better off getting your own set of offices and your own team to run them.'

Michael comes into PR from another career

Much of Michael Bryan's working life was spent in marketing and advertising for a blue chip company. He was over 40 when he decided to pack in his job and start up on his own in PR, together with a partner with whom he had worked in the same company – who did precisely the same thing.

He insists: 'I knew nothing about PR when I began, but I read every book I could on the subject and it really helped. Initially, my clients were small, with budgets to match, but because of them I gradually got to know and understand the media.

'As my media contacts developed, so did my client list. Today, I work out of central London offices with a team of three. I make a habit of calling media contacts regularly, even if I don't have something to 'sell'. That's because I believe the relationships you forge with the media, and the friendships you develop, are what makes PR work.

'We've worked very hard in the last seven years, but we make a good return on our investment. It's a better package than in my last company. I love what I do and have no regrets about making the move.'

SUMMARY

If you're going to be a freelancer you'll need to:

● get some experience first

● be exceptionally disciplined

● control office procedures.

8
Aiming to Specialise

Once you have some work experience behind you, you may well wish to specialise in a particular field of PR. An expert's knowledge is always in demand, and even if you have yet to acquire sufficient practical work experience, it is never too soon to consider what areas are most likely to interest you.

Specialised knowledge can be beneficial to the freelancer and the in-house employee, but there are also agencies which have built up reputations for certain kinds of accounts, like Lynn Franks, who successfully made herself and her business well known for fashion accounts. Reasons for specialising are likely to include the following:

- more money
- expert knowledge
- greater demand.

INVESTIGATING POSSIBLE AREAS

It is possible to specialise in almost any area, from fashion and beauty to travel or technical. To make it simple, there are five main areas you could aim to hone in on:

- consumer-led
- technical
- financial
- political
- personal publicity.

Consumer-led

This is the most popular area with those hoping to specialise, but also perhaps the easiest in which to gain knowledge reasonably quickly.

When we talk about consumer-led accounts, we are talking about subjects like beauty, fashion, food or travel . . . all of which are deemed to be glamorous. Indeed, they can be, but specialised knowledge in any of these areas is still not going to be gained overnight. That need to keep up to date will always be with you, as trends change over the years.

What aptitudes?

● Dedicated desire to learn about specific product area.

● Ability to keep in touch with changing trends.

● Interest in history and finite detail.

Technical

Technical PR is particularly sought after. The person who is able to understand, interpret and explain computer jargon, for example, will be worth their weight in gold to some companies. Obviously, it takes time to learn about any technical field, but not everyone has the talent or liking for this type of PR. Some college leavers who enter this field, flattered by salary offers, could soon find the topics they are dealing with unappealing.

What aptitudes?

● Attention to minute detail.

● Excellent memory for minutae.

● Love of making sense out of intricate technical jargon.

Financial

Financial PR is extremely highly sought after and perhaps one of the best paid areas. If you are in this field, it may mean you will deal with investors or shareholders as well as investment analysts and city editors. Work in financial PR more than likely includes preparation of annual reports and accounts; can involve shareholder information and/or loyalty schemes. Explanations of annual accounts, in layman's terms, are an obvious part of the job. These could be in the form of videos for employee intake.

Financial PR may well be part of an in-house PR's job with or without an outside specialist agency. City-based agencies, dealing only with financial PR, are likely to recruit from financial journalists or graduates qualified in related fields.

In the financial sphere, the product is a sensitive one which requires diplomacy. It is therefore a fair bet that a one-to-one relationship with influential media may well stand you in better stead than a flow of too much information to too many people. Stock exchange information is reliant on electronic media, so remember time differences around the world. Financial PR tends to make announcements which are concise and to the point, rather than 'frilly' releases.

It is possible to build a special PR exercise around an annual report, highlighting achievements perhaps in the past financial year, or explaining losses.

What aptitudes?

● Financial background.

● Analytical mind.

● Ability to assess financial situations.

● Diplomacy.

Political

Parliamentary PR is another highly specialised area in which a consultant might advise clients on parliamentary issues and interpret white or green papers, etc. When a company is constantly involved in political matters, it is likely to engage a full-time political PR person, but most companies only have occasional need of political PR and will call in an agency specialist on an *ad hoc* basis.

What aptitudes?

- Legal or business background.

- Interest in political affairs.

- Ability to put analysis into layman terms.

- Diplomacy.

Personal publicity

Being a publicist requires certain attitudes and type of character. Before aiming to be one, you should carefully consider the fields you love best. Is it show business, books, classical music, art? To do a good job publicising a person means loving the field which that person is in.

What aptitudes?

- Able to be on call 24-hours.

- Capable of handling temperamental people.

- Huge amount of energy.

- Calm temperament.

Courses to take

Any course that concentrates on financial or business areas lends itself to a later career in a specialised PR field. A history or arts degree may help later discipline when learning about a particular company's products and how they are made. Fashion, design and beauty training could give the edge when subsequently you are handling related products.

WOOING THE RIGHT PRESS

The specialist PR, more than any other, should have an intimate relationship with the media who matter. Wooing the right press doesn't mean buying them expensive lunches or giving lavish presents. It means giving them a story they can use, assisting with information wherever and whenever possible, perhaps granting them an exclusive occasionally and knowing them sufficiently well to ask for a favour when you need it.

To begin with some kind of personal contact, to put a face to a name, assess attitudes and requirements, is helpful.

> **Don't be misled into thinking you, the PR, needs the press more than they need you. When you are a specialist, the media needs you just as much.**

What publications?

As you will have read in Chapter 5, there are specialised journals and broadcast programmes for most fields and these will be your target markets. The basic questions are:

- What do I want to say?

- Who do I want to tell?

Along with those specialised journals, though, there will be others which could also be of use to you. You may have an account which relates to golf, for instance. Golf-only publications may be target market number one, but any media that deals with sport may be relevent: men's magazines, women's magazines, airline and hotel magazines, business travel magazines . . . the list is seemingly endless.

On the other hand, some media may not be right for your market. Will the readers of *The Sun* be likely to stay at that expensively deluxe five-star hotel? Does *Best* magazine ever run a restaurant review? Do you *want* your client featured on *Watchdog*?

Key questions to ask yourself

- Do I care about image?

- Is my product/service in a special niche market?

- Am I looking for as wide a spread of publicity as possible?

BECOMING AN EXPERT

It may happen by chance

With the ability to know the type of area which will ultimately most interest you, you can start to become an expert from square one. In all truth, though, most current PR experts fell into their specialism. They loved it, but had not necessarily decided upon it (see Case Studies).

Assessing the plus factors of specialising

- Opportunity to become a recognised expert.

- Chance to earn larger fees.

Assessing the pitfalls of specialising

- Restricted to narrow fields.

- Acceptance of lower fees if switching fields.

GIVING YOURSELF PR

This means making yourself known and being seen in the best possible light. Word of mouth reputation can't be beaten, of course, but there are two other ways to spread the word about yourself:

- advertising
- networking.

Advertising

There is no harm in advertising your speciality. Many PRs advertise to be in the *Hollis* directory and publications like *PR Week*. Journalists who specialise in certain fields, such as travel, often produce their own year book in which they invite PRs to advertise so that their members can see at a glance who does what.

Networking

Despite the fierce competition existing between rival PRs, there is also a tremendous camaraderie. Attending functions where other PRs are guests, or getting together on an informal basis, is no bad thing and can see business results. A PR will recommend another to a potential client or journalist when appropriate, perhaps for lack of time or resources.

REAPING THE REWARDS

The person who sets up their own specialised business and is prepared to work day and night at it can see it expand profitably before they reach 40.

CASE STUDIES

Maureen specialises in restaurants and chefs

Maureen Mills worked in PR and marketing for British Airways for eight-and-a-half years before becoming editor of *Where* magazine, a tourist publication featuring restaurants and nightlife. Two years ago she set up in business for herself, specialising in restaurants and chefs, using a dedicated office in her home.

'I work well independently and manage my time easily, perhaps because I have a background of big corporation framework. I don't need a central location or plush office style and I love the flexibility of working where I live. My day is not a nine-to-five one and I do come in for a couple of hours on weekends, which maybe is a downside because you're always aware the office is there. You can't exactly shut the door either mentally or physically, which you can do if your office is outside. I'm a workaholic but at home I can dip in and out of work as I wish . . . the other day I roasted a chicken while I was working, dressed in leggings and t-shirt rather than smart suit. I am also always here for deliveries.'

Maureen currently has some ten accounts, all restaurant related. 'Always stick with what you know, if you go it alone,' she says. 'By becoming a specialist, even more work comes your way. It's all about what you know, who you know and how good you are . . . work comes to me because of my contacts. Because I've worked on the other side I know what the media wants. I would only plug into other fields if I could kill three birds with one stone. I did do a one-off project in another area but it took me far longer to achieve results.

'I only deal with large corporations who have budgets and my passion for restaurants is always with me. It's true, I happened to start my company when there was a phenomenal boom in the UK. It's boom time for the business I've chosen. Maybe that won't be so in ten years' time.'

A few months ago, Maureen took on an assistant who works flexi-hours for her. 'She has a child and didn't want a full-time job. We work around each other which suits us both.'

She insists that the freelance PR who specialises can earn a lot of money. 'If you find a niche and have the contacts, you're on a winning ticket. But I haven't just dipped into this niche market and I do have North American experience, too. In my first year, I turned over £75,000; in the second I doubled that. I have had offers to finance my company's growth, merge with me and buy me out, but at the moment I love doing what I'm doing and how I'm doing it.'

Stella opts for show business publicism

Stella Wilson trained in classical ballet, was awarded an Arts Council bursory to study arts administration as a mature student and has worked in marketing and PR, always in art fields. Since 1984 she has specialised as a publicist. Her clients include Joan Collins, whom she frequently accompanies on publicity tours.

'The arts administration course (six months, five of which were placements) opened many doors in the arts field. I have always been interested in show business because I like creative people. Being a publicist gives me the chance to work with them. Doing "personal" publicity is not for everyone, but I like that involved, rather complex relationship that a publicist has with a client. I have never wished to expand my company because that personal attention would be lost. I would never want more than five clients at any one time for that very reason.

'To be a publicist you have to have huge energy and enormous patience because you're often dealing with temperamental people who can be under stress themselves and subsequently must be handled in a certain way. I see myself as a calming influence.

'My job is a 24-hour one. A publicist can't be unavailable whether it's 6 am or 1 am. I live on the phone. Every day I must receive around a dozen calls about Joan Collins alone, and make another twelve on her behalf for future projects. When you are dealing with such a well known celebrity, the publicity catchment area is that much wider. There is publicity whether or not you specifically like or want it.

'Unlike some publicists, I don't do stunts for clients, and publicity in a downmarket tabloid would not be good for the image of, say, a serious Shakespearian actress. Nevertheless, a publicist must know what makes a story or a phone call is wasted. I spent a couple of years on the *Cambridge Evening News* in the arts section, so I know what type of releases catch the eye, or get binned instead. Actually, I hardly ever write a release.

'A publicist may well have to fend off phone call requests for client information or interviews, but always nicely. Who knows where that journalist at the end of the phone line will end up? When I think a publication or story angle is unsuitable for a client, I have to say "no" as sweetly as possible. At other times, it is easy for me to answer questions on behalf of a client because I know that client's answers.

'In America, almost every celebrity has both an agent and a personal publicist. In the UK, it is more rare.'

Victoria establishes a successful hotel/travel group

Victoria Fuller began working as a secretary in the press office of Benetton, graduating to an assistant's position where, she says, 'I still made the tea'. Her luck of being in the right place at the right time gave her the opportunity to organise a series of regional fashion shows . . . the start of her real PR career.

After living for a while in Paris, she was hired by Regine to work in-house for the London Club, 'making sure the Dempseys of this world came to celebrity birthday parties, that kind of thing.' During that time, she became friends with the corporate membership secretary and when the club folded, the two of them decided to set up a small company in 1986.

'We did our first few hotel openings in 1987, the beginning of specialism PR, but we were still working out of home which meant no overheads. We realised that if we wanted to make the business work, we had to specialise. After all, if I were a client, I'd want to hire a specialist.'

Robert, whose background was city corporate finance, joined Victoria and her partner and they moved into a separate office in 1990, by which time the official company was known as ZFL. An assistant was recruited as account executive.

'Although my original partner, the "Z" in ZFL, had left as of 1991, we had become total hotel specialists and were looking towards Europe, a destination on everyone's lips. We recruited a PR from Leading Hotels of the World with this in mind, and in 1992 set up a separate division known as Columbus Communications.

'At first, everyone did everything, whichever division they worked for. That proved inoperable. Now, ZFL has eight hands-on employees, Columbus has five, servicing some twenty-eight clients across the group. Robert acts as financial director over both divisions and an accountant deals with both sets of books. Offices have been set up in Paris and Munich where nationals have been hired as employees.'

Of the group's twenty-eight clients, some are individual hotels, some are groups such as Four Seasons or Rafael, and the annual turnover is in excess of 1.2m. Victoria (now 33) is acting MD of ZFL but retains the majority of shares in Columbus Communications.

Says Victoria: 'We're always upfront with potential new clients that we operate two companies, both specialising in the same field. However, we explain that while they work under the same roof, they employ separate staff and telephone/fax numbers. Nowadays, ninety per cent of business comes through word of mouth because of our hands-on, personalised service and we believe that both divisions continue to offer that service at value for money.

'My main partner, Robert, and I possess different strengths

and weaknesses. I am not terribly good at finance; he is a little disorganised on the operational side. I believe a one-man-band would incur difficulties in a specialised situation which they would like to see grow because no one can service clients personally and pitch for new business at the same time.

'Specialising can mean good money, though I have to say the travel area is notoriously badly paid. The advantage of using a specialist agency is they know what they're talking about rather than those which have general purpose accounts. Because they're dealing with the same media time and time again, they may well be that medium's first port of call. When you specialise, you are given the chance of being the best in any given field and gain a degree of expertise by being especially focused on one area.

'I admit it narrows the field. Should the specialist want to switch fields, they might have to take a step back. But I still think it's worth it and the growth of our business seems to prove it.'

When it comes to hiring junior staff, Victoria says: 'It's a question of attitude. Degrees are not essential. Because I don't have one myself, I wouldn't rule someone else out because they didn't have one either. Organisational skills and presentation are what count. We have many graduates coming for interviews, but if they look as if they've just got out of bed and have a ring through their nose, it's a no immediately, even if they do have a First at Oxbridge. Yes, I do look for good looks, an outgoing personality and an amenable manner.

'We work with the BUNAC programme quite a lot – American students who spend six months working with us as part of practical experience for their degree – and we've found them to be excellent.'

SUMMARY

If you're going to specialise, make sure you:

- take a related course

- love the field

- think laterally about the field

- aim for the top.

9
Getting the First Foot in the Door

When Conrad Hilton talked about what made a successful hotel, he emphasised location, location, location. For a young person hoping to get a first foot in the PR door, the emphasis would be presentation, presentation, presentation.

With or without specific academic qualifications, care should be taken when making first enquiries; thought should be given to writing a CV and accompanying letter; and good appearance made at any ensuing interview.

MAKING FIRST ENQUIRIES

By studying copies of *PR Week* and the *Hollis* directory, you can create a shortlist of PR agencies you wish to approach. A phonecall enquiring about the possibility of a vacant position, or likely recruitment in the near future, doesn't harm, but always follow it up with a letter and CV. That, too, should be followed up with a further phonecall in a couple of weeks if there has been no response.

Writing the letter

Don't do a blanket mailing willy-nilly. Know to whom you are writing and why. Writing enthusiastically will aid your cause far more than a bland request for a job. Remember, that if you have no previous work experience, it is what the company can do for you (ie, teach the tricks of the trade) rather than vice versa.

Figure 7 shows examples of parts of letters sent to a medium-sized consultancy, with 'turn-down' results. These are obvious cases of not doing homework. The writers did not bother to find out the name of the person in charge. One phone call would

Dear Sir/Madam,

I would like to apply for any administrative/ office junior opening that you may currently have. As you can see from my enclosed CV, I have clerical experience, both in work and during my NVQ work placements for my Business Administration course.

I am hard working, well organised and able to work as part of a team.

Another example of failure to do homework is the following intro to a letter of application:

Dear Sir/Madam,

Having recently graduated in European Business, I am writing to see if you have any suitable vacancies. I am particularly interested in pursuing a career in Marketing and in becoming actively involved with the running of a Marketing Department.

As can be seen from my enclosed CV, I studied various areas of marketing in my degree. I am eager to further my knowledge in all areas of marketing, and feel that any theoretical knowledge I possess will prove beneficial.

Fig. 7. How not to write a letter of application.

have achieved it. Nor do the writers indicate whether they know the target is a PR consultancy or why they want to work in one.

Figure 8 shows a letter written by a young hopeful, who subsequently proved successful.

The writer here has taken the trouble to find out the top name to whom to write. While making no bones about his own talents, he nevertheless implies that he could not hope for more than a junior position. This kind of letter won the writer several interviews, and ultimately a job.

Summing up the ground rules

● Know who you are writing to.

● Know why you are writing to them.

● Write with enthusiasm, indicating your desire to work in the PR field.

Writing the CV

Providing you leave wide margins and double-space your CV, which should be word processed/printed, there is no set style. You might like to consider the following order of headings, however:

(a) Name, address and status
This should be your top heading, together with telephone number and followed by marital status.

(b) Aims and objectives
A short paragraph about what you are seeking to achieve through a career in PR might give the reader beneficial insight.

(c) Experience
If you have any work experience, start with the most recent and work backwards. Deal with part-time work/summer jobs and/or work experience gained as part of a degree course in the same way.

Dear Mr Brown,
I am writing to you as a graduate who is
committed to following a career in public
relations.

As you will see from my CV, I am a recent
graduate with excellent all-round ability
which, I feel, makes me ideally suited to the
multi-skilled world of PR. My previous
employment has honed my verbal and
communication skills and in all aspects I
have proven myself to be a dedicated team
player and an imaginative and accomplished
individual.

I am flexible and enthusiastic, and can back
this up with hard work, excellent
administrative and organisational skills,
and a keen eye for detail. Given the
opportunity, I am sure you would find me a
proficient and productive member of your
team. I am ideally seeking a junior position
in your ambitious and successful agency
where my industrious and creative nature can
blossom.

Fig. 8. Writing a good letter of application.

(d) Skills
Even if you have no work experience, you probably have some
skills worth mentioning here, such as computer knowledge,
book-keeping or other secretarial skills. These may have been
learnt on a short certificated or diploma course. Alternatively,
they may have been acquired as a hobby interest.

(e) Education
Under this heading you'll give your educational background,

starting from the most recent (eg, a degree) and descending in order.

(f) Personal details
Here, besides your date of birth, you may list interests and hobbies, club memberships, etc.

(g) References
If you have work experience, give the name and address of anyone you feel might write a favourable report on your behalf, if requested. Only two are necessary. Those without work experience may care to list a couple of personal referees, eg a teacher, to do similar. Alternatively, you may offer to supply references upon request.

A successful CV
Figure 9 is an example of a CV written by a successful applicant. Note that in this case, educational achievements were considered greater than actual work experience, and were therefore placed before Employment. You will also note that the applicant makes positive statements about 'Achievements and Interests', giving the impression of being a good all-rounder.

Attaching a photograph
A passport-sized headshot attached to your CV could be to your advantage. This is not to suggest that the peruser is looking for good looks, rather to say they may think they know what is a right look.

PRESENTING YOURSELF WELL

If you sent a letter and CV covered in ink or wine blots, it would give out signs you were careless. A handwritten CV would show lack of professional thought. The same goes for appearance. The person who is unkempt in dress could be perceived to be undisciplined in work, so a neat, clean appearance is paramount. Watch out for shoes – they're a giveaway. Many interviewers have been impressed by manner and mode of an interviewee until regarding dirty and scuffed footwear.

None of this means you have to look formal and stuffy. After

CV

Name

Address

Personal details

Profile Ambitious graduate in Tourism and Planning. An effective thinker with proven communications skills. Able to work productively as part of a team whilst displaying initiative and enterprise.

Education
1993–97 Oxford Brookes University BA Honours (Modular) Degree in Tourism & Planning.

1989–91 Mander, Portman & Woodward College A Levels: Economics (A) Environmental science (B) English (C)

1986–89 Reigate Grammar School 9 O Levels

Employment
1997/98 Business Development Executive, General Question, Oxford.
Initially working as a telephone interviewer, was given a supervisory role, responsible for briefing and training temps. Promoted to executive position for the 3M Commercial Graphics sales team, covering the UK and Ireland and responsible for own department's admin and organisation.

1997 Temporary positions with agencies, calling for flexibility, reliability and commitment. Work included market research.

Fig. 9. Writing a good CV.

1995	Brochure Production Coordinator First Choice Holidays, Sussex (summer job). Coordinated production of 230-page holiday brochure from conception to print. Arranged photo shoots, wrote copy, liaised with resorts, designers, printers and marketing.
1994	General Assistant, The Oxford Story, Oxford (summer job). Performed a supervisory role serving and dealing with many nationalities.
1989	Publicity Assistant for Hulse Communications, helping out with media and client liaison, research and analysis and launch events.

Achievements and Interests
- Widely travelled, including ten months living abroad 1992/93. Good knowledge of written and spoken French.

- Computer literate with good working knowledge of Word, Windows, Filemaker Pro, Powerpoint, Excel and the Internet on IBM and Apple Mac computers, with fast accurate keyboard skills.

- Clean driving licence and car owner.

- Captain of school cricket team and colours for rugby and soccer. Qualified open water diver (PADI)

- Arranged and organised profit-making New Year party for 300 in Reigate, 1994.

- Responsible for the promotion and organisation of events for the Live Music Society, Oxford Brookes University.

- General interests include travel, modern drama, current affairs, sport, music, classic cars, cookery.

References
Available upon request.

Fig. 9. Continued.

all, a company or agency specialising in fashion would expect you to dress in current style, and appreciate personal touches.

A good conversationalist is bound to find an interview easier than the person who can't stop the erms and ahs. Be sure to talk about your own aspirations, but be a good listener, too. Be economical with the truth rather than lie and turn what could sound a negative answer into a positive one. For example, don't say 'I've never worked with Windows.' Instead, say 'I've worked on a computer so I'm sure I'd soon be *au fait* with Windows.'

WHAT ARE THE QUALIFICATIONS

A diploma or degree in media studies, PR, business studies or any related subject can undoubtedly give you an edge over the competition. But the 'way in' is what you want to make of it, as you'll see from the three case studies at the end of the chapter.

TAKING A COURSE

There are ways of acquiring a higher education without opting for a degree course.

HNCs and HNDs

Higher National Certificate (HNC) and Higher National Diploma (HND) courses are offered by many colleges and universities these days. These vocational courses are generally related to a particular career area, such as business studies or tourism studies. HNDs are made up of units of study and usually take two years full-time. HNCs are generally taken part-time by those already in work.

DipHEs and NVQs

Some universities and colleges offer a full-time two-year Diploma of Higher Education (DipHE) which equates to the first two years of a degree course, but they're few and far between. Higher Level National Vocational Qualifications (NVQs) are designed for those working at supervisory or management level.

Allied subjects

You will be lucky to find a non-degree course in public relations *per se*, but allied subjects such as media studies or marketing are readily available (eg: through City & Guilds).

Finding out more

If you are having a problem finding out where you can take a short course, check with your local education authority. Most careers offices and schools, along with some libraries, will have access to ECCTIS, an information service covering courses available in Universities and Colleges of Higher and Further Education. It is also available on CD Rom for use on pcs and on the Invernet.

STUDYING FOR A DEGREE

If you wish to apply for a full-time or sandwich degree course at a UK University or College of Higher Education, you must do so through UCAS. Application forms and handbooks are available from colleges, careers offices or from UCAS itself (see Useful Addresses).

The application form allows you to list six choices of institutions and courses. If you are applying to one institution only you can, if you wish, apply for more than one course.

Entry requirements

Entry requirements vary as much by course as with your age and stage. UCAS annually publishes a directory listing requirements for all courses in the scheme. Reference copies are available in colleges, career services and public libraries.

When to apply

Applications are generally made in the autumn before entering higher education, with a closing date of December 15th in most cases. The sooner you apply, the more likelihood of an available place.

After applying

Each institution of your choice will consider your application independently of the others, sending their decision on to you via UCAS.

- If the offer made is **unconditional**, it means the institution is happy to admit you.

- If the offer is **conditional**, you will need to satisfy whatever conditions are required before your place can be confirmed.

- You are allowed to accept one conditional offer firmly, implying your commitment to go to that institution once you have satisfied its conditions.

- You may also hold one other offer as insurance. If you do not meet the conditions of the firm offer, but do meet those of the insurance, you will be placed at the latter choice.

- If you receive no offers, or fail conditions, there is another opportunity called **clearing**, which takes place July, August and September. This is when UCAS publishes information about still-available vacancies.

Applying for grants and loans

Since almost every institution charges an enrolment fee, higher education doesn't exactly come cheaply, but you may find you're eligible for a grant. Your best bet is to write to your local education authority (LEA) for a free copy of *Student Grants and Loans: A brief guide*, or alternatively from the Publications Dispatch Centre of the Department for Education and Employment (see Useful Addresses). You should apply to the LEA for an award subject as soon as you have applied to an institution through UCAS.

Applying in Scotland
Application for student's allowance should be made to the Student Awards Agency for Scotland (see Useful Addresses).

Loans
Providing you meet personal and eligible course requirements, you are entitled to a student loan to help meet living costs while

studying. This government-funded system allows you to borrow money at a rate of interest linked to inflation and offers additional financial support even if you are awarded a grant.

Loan amounts will vary depending upon where you live/study, and are lower in the final year of study.

Eligibility
Normally, personal eligibility means you must have resided in the UK for at least three years prior to starting your course and be aged under 50. Eligible courses are offered by:

- universities
- higher education colleges
- Scottish grant-aided colleges
- certain private and NHS college courses
- other publicly funded institutions which provide higher education courses.

Loan agreements are not based on either your or your parents' financial circumstances. Loan repayments begin in the April after completing your course unless your gross income is below eighty-five per cent of the national average, in which case you can request a deferment for twelve months at a time.

Scholarships and sponsorship
Some institutions have a small number of scholarships which are listed in their prospectuses.

Sponsorship enables employers seeking promising recruits to begin training at an earlier stage than waiting for course completion. Full details to be available opportunities are to be found in the booklet *Sponsorship for Students*, published by the Careers and Occupational Information Centre (COIC), available from most school careers and public libraries, as well as local careers advisory company offices.

Overseas students
Information and advice about UK higher education and suitability of qualifications can be obtained from your nearest British Council office which should hold reference material. Your own country's education authorities, the nearest British Embassy or

High Commission, are other sources of information, and may be able to answer questions about grants and scholarships.

Unless you are an EC student, expect enrolment fees to be considerably higher than those charged to UK residents.

CASE STUDIES

Crispin's homework pays off

Crispin, aged 24, took a three-year degree course in International Relations in Sussex. Course topics covered policy making, international history and international political theory. Out of term jobs included a short stint at Selfridges.

'It was my career advisor who suggested I investigate areas to do with PR, marketing and communications,' he explains. 'I went to the library and made a list of medium-sized agencies with fifty-plus employees along with the type of accounts they dealt with.

'Directory listings are expensive for a student to buy, so I went to my local reference library and picked out ten names of companies to be sent a letter and CV. I used a colour laser copier to reproduce my CV and show a colour headshot in one corner.

'Phonecalls ascertained which agencies offered training schemes and/or work experience. One which offered the latter took me on for a month after a quick chat. Really, I was an administrative dogsbody so I learnt very little, but then one of the full-time employees left and there I was, in the right place at the right time. Because I had shown enthusiasm, I was hired.

'Now, almost a year has gone by and I work as part of a team in charge of several accounts and am considered a trainee account executive. That means I go along with the team when they pitch for a new account and am involved in existing projects. I like the variety and if my appraisals continue to be good, hope to make a career here.'

Jo's PR degree pays dividends

Jo, now 26, opted for one of the first PR degrees at Leeds Business School. She confesses: 'I had thought to do European business studies with French, but that course was full. PR with French, however, was available.

'I could have done a four-year degree, the last year as work experience, but thought by cutting it to three years I'd be a step ahead of the others. Even so, you are sent off to a local consultancy for an afternoon every two weeks to make hands-on use of theory. The course I did covered a general grounding in business, accounting and computing so it was useful whichever way you looked at it.

'During the degree course, subjects covered included writing news releases, crisis management, design, writing corporate brochures and, through that, some involvement with printing. Some of the projects were 'live', like that in my final year: a six months' communications audit which had to be presented to the Board of the Business School upon completion.

'PR was a new degree course when I took it at Leeds, so both teachers and students were on a learning curve. Professional PRs were brought in to lecture us about possible situations and how they dealt with them.

'After I finished my degree, I selected twenty consultancies in the area and wrote them a letter advising them that I had just achieved a PR degree. The response was excellent and I was offered work immediately. I was able to take a portfolio of work I'd done as part of the course, such as student newsletters, with me to interviews and everyone seemed to appreciate it. Perhaps the response was so good because of the novelty of a PR degree.

'I spent two-and-a-half years working in technological PR, but it wasn't my cup of tea. So when I moved to London, I chose to work for a one-man-band on the consumer side, despite being headhunted by large agencies who wanted me for my technology experience. As a right-hand assistant I get to talk to the consumer press, write releases and really get my hands into a project. Ultimately, I would like to move on to a bigger consultancy dealing with consumer accounts.'

Tom's degree is only the starting point

Tom, aged 25, recently came through a three-year degree course in tourism and planning with a BA honours degree 'I thought I had to get a degree to find a decent job, and tourism had always interested me because I felt it would lead to plenty of personal travel, which I love.

'Initially, I kept a strict eye on want ads in *The Guardian* and

PR Week. My idea was if they were recruiting at the top end, they would be bound to have to recruit lower down sooner or later. I was shortlisted for interviews four times using such methods.

'My letter seemed to get me response, but six interviews later I still hadn't got a job. I changed my letter approach from one of "I'd really like to work for you" to a more aggressive "This is what I can do." I became more pro-active.

'The real reason I didn't get jobs was down, I believe, to lack of work experience in the PR field. But then, suddenly I had two simultaneous offers, one from a very large consultancy as campaign assistant and one from a far smaller consultancy whose clients are mostly travel related.

'I chose the latter and have been hired on a six-month trial basis. I deal with press phone enquiries, write releases, research information, write captions, send out trannies, all in all get to do a bit of everything. I am hoping that my appraisal will be good enough to allow me to stay.'

SUMMARY

To get that first foot in the door be sure to:

- consider degree or other courses carefully

- make selective applications

- show enthusiasm

- think out your presentation.

10
Looking at Courses

It may seem strange, since public relations is such a popular career area, but very few institutions offer public relations courses *per se*. You won't, for instance, find such a City & Guilds course. Even when it comes to degrees, the 1998 UCAS handbook lists just four universities offering specialised PR degree courses. If you are convinced that a career in PR *is* what you want it is worth considering any of these four, as opposed to taking some other, unrelated degree. The universities are:

Bournemouth University
Talbot Campus
Fern Barrow
Poole
Dorset BH12 5BB
Tel: (01202) 525111.

University of Central
   Lancashire
Preston PR1 2HE
Tel: (01772) 201201.

Leeds Metropolitan University
Calverley Street
Leeds LS1 3HE
Tel: (0113) 283 3113.

The University College of St
   Mark & St John
Derriford Road
Plymouth
Devon PL6 8BH
Tel: (01752) 636827.

WHAT CAN YOU EXPECT FROM A DEGREE COURSE?

A degree course will introduce you to both the theory and practice of public relations. In addition to guest lecturers, you will be given projects and, in the best cases, work placement will form part of the course.

The following illustrate the 1998 course content of three universities offering PR degree courses.

BA (Hons) Public Relations, Bournemouth

Offered by Bournemouth University, this claims to be the only sandwich honours degree of its kind available in the UK. One of its key features is a full year's placement with employers like British Airways, Harrods, Revlon as well as consultancies.

How to enter
Grades are given points:

- an A pass = 10 points
- a B = 8 points
- a C = six points, etc.

You will need to have acquired twenty points from A level passes. Any equivalent combination of A and AS levels will also suffice.

Course content

- **Year 1**
— PR theory and practice
— Political and economic analysis
— Media and society
— Marketing principles and practice
— Writing: foundation skills
— Applied research methods.

- **Year 2**
— PR programmes
— PR environments
— Written and visual communications
— Persuasions and influence
— Communication in groups
— Business context.

- **Year 3**
— Supervised forty-week placement in a public relations consultancy or an in-house public relations department.

- **Year 4**
— Dissertation
— Issues management and social responsibility
— Organisations: behaviour and communication.

- **Options** (select 2)
— Marketing public relations
— Advertising
— Investor relations
— Public affairs
— International public relations
— Strategic management and organisation.

BA (Hons) Public Relations, Lancashire

The University of Central Lancashire was one of the first universities to introduce public relations at degree level.

How to enter
Entrance here requires eighteen points through A level passes, with a good standard of written English. The three-year full-time degree course comes under the Department of Journalism.

Course content
This course is divided into two stages: stage one covers the first year, stage two years two and three. In each year, students normally take six modules.

- **Stage 1** comprises five compulsory modules:
— Public relations in society
— Media awareness
— Journalism practice 2
— Introduction to media
— Communications
— Introduction to business.

The sixth module is elective whereby students may make a free choice from the University Electives Catalogue.

- **Stage 2** comprises five compulsory modules and a sixth elective one, for year two.

— Public relations practice 1
— Public relations practice 2
— Attitude, persuasion and influence
— Strategic communications
— Practical public relations (placement/work experience).

● **Compulsory third year modules**
— Public relations practice 3
— Advanced public relations techniques
— Corporate and financial PR
— Public affairs
— Dissertation.

● **Option modules** include:
— Specialist PR
— Multicultural PR
— Introduction to marketing management
— Ethics and management
— Journalism issues
— Journalism design.

BA (Hons) Public Relations, Leeds

A three-year full-time or four-year sandwich course is offered by Leeds School of Business Strategy, Beckett Park Campus.

How to enter
Normal entry requirements apply, though an A level in English is a preferred pass. As part of this degree, there is an opportunity to study a European language.

Course content

● **Level 1** subjects include:
— Introduction to public relations theory and practice
— Introduction to information technology
— Business accounting
— Mass communication
— People and organisations and economic awareness, or a language.

- **Level 2** subjects include:
— PR planning and management
— PR practice
— Psychology
— Philosophy and politics
— Marketing
— Research methods.

For those taking a language, a period of study abroad is included.

- **Sandwich year**
— Optional work placement with a consultancy or in-house department.

- **Level 3**
— Dissertation
— Group project
— Corporate relations
— PR practice
— Business.

POSTGRADUATE/DIPLOMA COURSES IN PR

The following universities offer the above, recommended by the Institute of Public Relations (IPR).

College	Course
University of Stirling Stirling FK9 4LA Tel: (01786) 466220.	MSc in Public Relations 1 year full-time
Manchester Metropolitan University All Saints Manchester MI5 6BH Tel: (0161) 247 6050.	MA Public Relations 1 year full-time.
West Herts College Hempstead Road Watford	Postgraduate Diploma International Public Relations 1 year full-time.

Hertfordshire WD1 3EZ
Tel: (01923) 812622.

University of Wales
Heath park
Cardiff CF4 4XN
Tel: (01222) 874000.

Postgraduate Diploma
Public and Media Relations
2 terms full-time + 200 hours
   work placement.

QUALIFICATIONS VIA CAM

The Communication Advertising and Marketing Education Foundation awards certificates and diplomas that could be worth trying for, and which are an accepted qualification for associate IPR membership. CAM qualifications are set out to reflect the best practice in business in Europe.

How do I apply?

Examinations for the Certificate are held twice a year, in June and November, while exams for the Diploma are held only in June. Candidates applying for a CAM Certificate must have a minimum GCE/GCSE (or equivalent) pass in English or Maths. Those educated in the UK must also have achieved one of the following levels of qualification (or equivalent):

- A degree from a recognised university.

- A BTEC/SCOTVEC certificate or diploma in business studies.

- Two A levels and 3 GCSE passes grades A, B or C.

- Five GCSE passes (or equivalent) and relevant employment for at least one year.

- The London Chamber of Commerce and Industry third level group diploma in advertising, marketing and public relations.

Candidates who have passed in four Certificate subjects are then eligible to register for the Diploma.

THE CAM CERTIFICATE COURSE

Course content

Marketing
The syllabus will help you develop a knowledge of marketing and its role in business and society. Elements covered include:

- definition of marketing
- concept
- legal and environmental constraints
- market planning
- target marketing
- research
- product life cycle
- marketing mix
- financial aspects
- control and application.

Advertising
This segment will show you how advertising works in society and how it functions as a method of marketing communication as well as how it is controlled. Elements covered include:

- organisation
- types of advertising
- professional bodies
- function
- agencies
- media independents
- media owners
- campaign planning and development
- budgets, creation and production.

Public relations
This sector demonstrates how different 'publics' or markets may be reached. Elements covered include:

- history
- definition

- codes of practice
- management
- internal PR
- external PR
- techniques
- media production
- events, functions, promotions
- planning and programming
- crisis management.

Media

This part helps you to understand major media and its functions and includes research, technology and opportunities to be exploited by creativity. Elements covered include:

- media range and scope
- creativity
- media research
- planning.

Sales promotion and direct marketing

This segment demonstrates the roles of both sales promotion and direct marketing within the marketing function. Elements covered include:

- definitions
- research
- planning
- creating and producing
- controls.

Research and behavioural studies

This element studies the theories of market research and behavioural studies, applying them to marketing communications and sales practice. Elements covered include:

- communication context of research/behavioural study
- psychology
- sociology
- management

- market research techniques
- planning and application.

THE CAM DIPLOMA

To obtain this, you must pass in management and stratgey plus two other related papers if seeking to go into PR or advertising.

Course content

The compulsory management and strategy section demonstrates business management, practice and strategy and how it applies to the communications and related industries. Elements covered include:

- organisational structure
- financing
- planning objectives
- strategic audit
- positioning and uses of research
- practice
- recruitment and development
- resource evaluation
- application.

You then have a choice of:

- public relations practice
- public relations management
- consumer advertising
- business to business advertising
- sales promotion and direct marketing.

For the PR aspirant there are two appropriate papers:

Public relations: management
Elements covered include:

- public sector
- non-profit sector
- management, opportunities and constraints

- PR contribution
- PR specifics.

Public relations: practice
For this paper, all the techniques of the management exercise will be called upon. Essentially, this is an applications module.

Colleges offering CAM courses

College	Course
Aberdeen College Gallowgate Aberdeen AB9 1DN Tel: (01224) 612500.	Certificate and Diploma part-time.
Matthew Boulton College Hope Street Birmingham B5 7DB Tel: (0121) 446 4545.	Certificate and Diploma part-time (evenings) weekends (diploma).
Bracknell & Wokingham College Church Road Bracknell Berkshire RG12 1DJ Tel: (01344) 420411.	Certificate and Diploma part-time
Cambridge Marketing College St John's Innovation Centre Cowley Road Cambridge CB4 4WS Tel: (01223) 421903.	Certificate and Diploma (weekends)
Carshalton College Nightingale Road Carshalton Surrey SM5 3EJ.	Certificate part-time (evenings and Saturdays)
Eureka Training 4 Mitre Street Cheltenham Gloucestershire GL53 7DS Tel: (0181) 770 6795.	Certificate (Saturdays only)

Chippenham College   Certificate full-time
Cocklebury Road   Diploma part-time
Chippenham
Wiltshire SN15 3QD
Tel: (01249) 444501.

Stevenson College   Certificate
Bankhead Avenue   part-time
Sighthill
Edinburgh EH11 4DE
Tel: (0131) 535 4600.

Central College of Commerce   Certificate
300 Cathedral Street   part-time
Glasgow G1 2TA
Tel: (0141) 552 3941.

Procom College   Certificate and Diploma
25 St Andrews Road   (weekends)
Henley-on-Thames RG9 1HY
Tel: (01491) 572086.

YORACT   Certificate
Trinity & All Saints College   part-time
Leeds
Tel: (01274) 820444.

Hetherington Associates   Certificate
University of Northumbria   part-time
Newcastle
Tel: (0191) 410 7252.

University of Wales   Certificate and Diploma
Allt-Yr-Yn-Campus   part-time and evenings
POB 180
Newport
Gwent NP9 5XR
Tel: (01633) 432366.

Nottingham Community   Certificate
  College   part-time or modular
Carlton Road

Nottingham NG3 2NR
Tel: (01159) 101455.

Highbury College	Certificate
Cosham	part-time
Portsmouth PO6 2SA	
Tel: (01705) 283287.	

Procom Associates	Certificate and Diploma
Reading College of Technology	(weekends)
Reading	
Berkshire	
Tel: (01491) 572086.	

Redhill Business School	Certificate
East Surrey College	part-time
Claremont Road	
Gatton Point	
Redhill	
Surrey RH1 2JX	
Tel: (01737) 770348.	

Rugby College	Certificate
Lower Hillmorton Road	semi-correspondence
Rugby	
Warwickshire CV21 3QS	
Tel: (01788) 541666.	

Swansea College	Certificate
Tycoch Road	part-time
Tycoch	(day release)
Swansea SA4 9EB	
Tel: (01792) 284000.	

West Kent College	Certificate
Brook Street	part-time
Tonbridge	
Kent TN9 2PW	
Tel: (01732) 358101.	

Richmond upon Thames	Certificate
College	part-time
Egerton Road	

Twickenham TW2 7SJ
Tel: (0181) 607 8101.

Brooklands College   Certificate
Heath Road   part-time
Weybridge
Surrey KT13 8TT
Tel: (01932) 853300.

Lansdowne College   Certificate
40–44 Bark Place   full- and part-time
London W2 4AT   (evenings and day release)
Tel: (0171) 616 4410.

London College of FE   Certificate and Diploma
186 Clapham High Street   full-time, part-time and day
London SW4 7UG   release
Tel: (0171) 498 4819.

London College of Printing &   Certificate
  Distributive Trades   part-time (evenings)
65 Davies Street
London W1Y 2DA
Tel: (0171) 514 6500.

London Guildhall University   Certificate
84 Moorgate   part-time
London EC2M 6SQ.

Magdalen House Ltd   Certificate and Diploma
Premier House   full- and part-time
10 Gretcoat Place
London SW1P 1SB
Tel: (0171) 222 8866.

Martran College   Certificate
15 Macklin Street   full- and part-time
Covent Garden   Diploma (evenings)
London WC2B 5NH
Tel: (0171) 419 4400.

Westminster College   Certificate
Business School   part-time
Vincent Square   (evenings and half-day release)

London SW1P 2PD
Tel: (0171) 931 7317.

ALLIED COURSES

The number of allied courses are so many and varied that it would be impossible to list all of them here. The main topics you might consider when applying for a related course, are:

- advertising
- business studies
- communications
- journalism
- marketing
- media studies
- tourism.

In addition to degree courses in these subjects, Higher National Diploma (HND) courses are frequently available and are generally shorter. They are often two years full-time, though entry requirements are normally the same as for degrees.

GRADUATE TRAINEE PROGRAMMES

The following companies take on graduates, as trainees, from time to time. Applications should be made in writing.

Cohn & Wolfe
Communications House
48 Leicester Square
London WC2H 7LJ.

Burston-Marsteller Ltd
24/28 Bloomsbury Way
London EC1A 2PX.

Manning Salvage & Lee
123 Buckingham Palace Road
Victoria
London SW1W 9SH.

Fleishman-Hillard
25 Wellington Street
Covent Garden
London WC2E 7DA.

Harvard Public Relations
Harvard House
Summerhouse Lane
Harmondsworth
West Drayton
Middlesex UB7 0AW.

Dewe Rogerson
(Financial PR)
3 London Wall Buildings
London Wall
London EC2M 5SY.

Hill & Knowlton Ltd
5–11 Theobalds Road
London WC1X 8SH.

Shandwick Communications
  Ltd
114 Cromwell Road
London SW7 4ES.

Citigate Communications Ltd
26 Finsbury Square
London
EC2 1DS.

Biss Lancaster Plc
69 Monmouth Street
London WC2H 9DG.

Countrywide Porter Novelli
Bowater House
68 Knightsbridge
London SW1X 7LH.

TTA Public Relations &
  Marketing Consultants
Webb House
6 Burnell Road
Sutton
Surrey SM1 4BW.

Glossary

Annual report. An end of year summary of a company's financial results.

Background briefing. Giving the media (verbally and/or in press release form) any relevant history leading to a situation or event.

Broadcast material. Any feature material suited to airing on radio, usually supplied on tape.

Column inches. Space in a publication allotted to relevant client/company. Sometimes valued in terms of advertising value.

Communications. The methods by which information can be relayed.

Contacts. Influential media relevant to specific areas of interest.

Contact report. The summary of major meetings (often monthly), showing what has to be done, by whom and when.

Corporate gift. A promotional gift for media giveaway, designed to heighten awareness of a new product or service.

Corporate brochure. A brochure designed to raise company profile by stating facts and figures, usually reflecting both history and future prospects.

Crisis management. The skill and ability to handle press and public should a crisis situation arise.

Deadline. The day when a publication goes to press, ie when all material must be in hand.

Embargo. A specified time and date before which information is not available for release.

Endorsement. Written/verbal approval of a product/service by a respected personality or organisation.

Evaluation. The check on whether the aims and objectives of work done met and fulfilled the client's goals.

Fam trip. Short form for familiarisation trip to inspect facilities. Also known as **press trip** or **media visit**.

Feature material. Journalistic copy/tape production that may be used as is by the media, if desired.

Follow-up. The check to see if, when and how information provided to the media was used.

Gimmick. An innovative way to create attention.

Glossies. Upmarket magazines.

Hack. Colloquial word for a journalist.

Headline. A leading phrase to sum up news content.

Leak. An unofficial provision of information.

Lobbying. Bringing pressure to bear on a political situation.

Mail shot. A blanketed piece of literature whose aim is to elicit response.

Marketing services. PR backup support services to heighten awareness of a product/service, often by means of advertising, direct mail, etc.

Media facility. The method by which the media may more easily acquire/report information.

Media training. Training the client/company executive in preparation for a media interview.

Networking. Informal socialising in the interest of work.

News release. Written information of a newsworthy nature, sent to the media.

Off the record. Unattributable information relayed to the media for their benefit, often of a background nature.

One-to-one. Arrangement for one media representative to conduct an interview.

Personality. A well known celebrity in any field.

Photocall. Advance notice of a photo opportunity for press photographers.

Photo library. A 'bank' of pictures in photograph, transparency or CD Rom form from which a media representative may request a selection.

Photoshoot. PR-organised photography session.

Pitch. Seeking business by approaching a potential client or responding to client need to hire a PR agency, pitching for an account.

Position statement. A press statement frequently used after a crisis, dispute, takeover, etc.

Press conference. A meeting called to impart news information to the media.

Press cuttings. Clips from publications mentioning a relevant client/company.

Presenter. A TV or radio programme introducer.

Presentation. The method by which information is relayed to the media, frequently a combination of speech with visuals.

Proof-reading. Ensuring no errors occur in written work prior to it being printed.

Proposal. Written aims and objectives summary on behalf of a potential client, usually submitted by a shortlisted agency.

Qs and As. Briefing an executive about likely questions from the media at a conference and supplying possible answers.

Qualities. Upmarket newspapers.

Recharged costs. Costs incurred which are over and above an agreed fee, such as a launch party, printwork, etc, which are then charged back to the client.

Ring-round. Sounding out journalists by phone as to their interest in a specific event/invitation/interview/news story.

Spin doctor. PR adviser, particularly in vogue in the political world.

Spokesperson. Any official PR granted the authority to speak on behalf of an individual or company.

Sussing. Assessing a situation/publication/journalist.

Tabloids. Mass market newspapers.

Tender. The fee an agency would charge for an accepted proposal.

Trannies. Short for transparencies, colour images ready for colour separation/reproduction.

Video release. A short promotional video to visually enhance awareness of a product/service.

Further Reading

INTRODUCTORY, PRACTICAL AND GENERAL

Cosmopolitan Guide to Working in PR and Advertising, Robert Gray and Julia Hobsbawm (Penguin Books, 1996).

Effective Media Relations, Michael Bland, Alison Theaker and David Wragg (Kogan Page, 1996).

The Essentials of Public Relations, Sam Black (Kogan Page, 1993).

How to Understand and Manage Public Relations, Dr Jon White (Century Business, 1991).

The Management and Practice of Public Relations, Norman Stone (Macmillan Business, 1995).

Planning and Managing a Public Relations Campaign, Anne Gregory (Kogan Page, 1996).

The Practice of Public Relations, Sam Black (Butterworth Heinemann New, 4th ed. 1995).

Public Relations in Practice, Anne Gregory (Kogan Page, 1996).

Risk Issues and Crisis Management, Michael Register and Judy Larkin (Kogan Page, 1997).

Surviving the Media Jungle, Dina Ross (Pitman, 1990).

Teach Yourself Public Relations, Harvey J. Smith (Hodder & Stoughton, 1995).

TECHNIQUES AND SPECIALIST AREAS

The Communications Challenge – Personnel and PR perspectives, Theon Wilkinson (Institute of Personnel Management, 1989).

The Corporate Image, Nicholas Ind (Kogan Page, 2nd ed. 1992).

Ed's Financial Public Relations, Richard Bing and Pat Bowman (Butterworth Heinemann, 2nd ed. 1993).
Evaluating Press Coverage, David Phillips (Kogan Page, 1992).
International Public Relations, Sam Black (Kogan Page, 1993).
Public Relations in Practice – A casebook, Danny Moss (Routledge, 1990).
Sponsorship, Steve Sleight (McGraw Hill, 1989).

ANNUALS

Financial Times Public Relations Yearbook (Financial Times with the Public Relations Consultants Association).
Hollis Press and Public Relations Annual (Hollis).
Hollis Europe (Hollis).

PERIODICALS

The Institute of Public Relations Journal (four issues a year, IPR).
PR Week (weekly).
Press Gazette (weekly).

Useful Addresses

Communication Advertising and Marketing Education Foundation, Abford House, 15 Wilton Road, London SW1V 1NJ. Tel: (0171) 828 7506.

City & Guilds (Information), 1 Giltspur Street, London EC1A 9DD. Tel: (0171) 294 2468.

Department for Education and Employment, Honeypot Lane, Cannons Park, Stanmore, Middlesex HA7 1AZ.

Institute of Public Relations, The Old Trading House, 15 Northburgh Street, London EC1V 0PR. Tel: (0171) 253 5151.

London Chamber of Commerce & Industry, 33 Queen Street, London EC4. Tel: (0171) 248 4444.

Public Relations Consultants Association, Willow House, Willow Place, London SW1. Tel: (0171) 233 6026.

Student Awards Agency for Scotland, Gyleview House, 3 Redheughs Rigg, South Gyle, Edinburgh EH12 9AH.

UCAS (Universities and Colleges Admission Services), Fulton House, Jessop Avenue, Cheltenham, Gloucestershire GL50 3SH. Tel: (01242) 222444.

Index

HOW TO MARKET YOURSELF
A practical guide to winning at work

Ian Phillipson

In today's intensely competitive workplace it has become ever more vital to market yourself effectively, whether as a first-time job hunter, existing employee, or mature returner. This hard-hitting manual provides a really positive step-by-step guide to assessing yourself, choosing the right personal image, identifying and presenting the right skills, building confidence, marketing yourself in person and on paper, organising your self-marketing campaign, using mentors at work, selling yourself to colleagues, clients and customers, and marketing yourself for a fast-changing future. The book is complete with assignments and case studies.

160pp. illus. 1 85703 160 1.

GETTING INTO FILMS AND TELEVISION
Foreword by Sir David Puttnam

Robert Angell

Would you like to make a career in films or television? Whether you want to direct feature films, photograph documentaries, edit commercials or pop videos, write current affairs programmes for television, do artwork for animation or just know that you want to be involved in film or television in some capacity but are not quite sure how to set about getting started, this book will give you a wealth of information to guide you through the dense but exotic jungle of these exciting industries. 'Readable and useful.' *Amateur Film and Video Maker.* 'An indepth coverage of the subject. Offers a wealth of useful advice and addresses for more information . . . One of the essential references for careers libraries.' *The Careers Officer Journal.* 'A comprehensive guide in lay language . . . Each section includes suggested starting points for newcomers.' *BAFTA News.* 'You'll find all the answers to your questions in Robert Angell's book.' *Film Review.* Robert Angell is a Council Member of the British Academy of Film & Television Arts (BAFTA) and Chairman of its Programme Committee and Short Film Award jury.

168pp. illus. 1 85703 370 1. 4th edition.

PASSING THAT INTERVIEW
Your step-by-step guide to achieving success

Judith Johnstone

Everyone knows how to shine at interview – or do they? When every candidate becomes the perfect clone of the one before, you have to have that extra 'something' to raise you chances above the rest. Using a systematic and practical approach, this How To book takes you step-by-step through the essential pre-interview groundwork, the interview encounter itself, and what you can learn from the experience afterwards. The book contains sample pre- and post-interview correspondence, and is complete with a guide to further reading, glossary of terms, and index. 'This is from the first class How To Books stable.' *Escape Committee Newsletter*. 'Offers a fresh approach to a well documented subject.' Newscheck (*Careers Service Bulletin*). 'A complete step-by-step guide.' *The Association of Business Executives*. Judith Johnstone is a Member of the Institute of Personnel & Development; she has been an instructor in Business Studies and adult literacy tutor, and has long experience of helping people at work.

144pp. illus. 1 85703 360 4. 4th edition.

WRITING A CV THAT WORKS
Developing and using your key marketing tool

Paul McGee

What makes a CV stand out from the crowd? How can you present yourself in the most successful way? This practical book shows you how to develop different versions of your CV for every situation. Reveal your hidden skills, identify your achievements and learn how to communicate these successfully. Different styles and uses for a CV are examined, as you discover the true importance of your most powerful marketing tool. Paul McGee is a freelance Trainer and Consultant for one of Britain's largest out-placement organisations. He conducts Marketing Workshops for people from all walks of life.

128pp. illus. 1 85703 365 5. 2nd edition.

GETTING THAT JOB
The complete job finders handbook

Joan Fletcher

Now in its fourth edition this popular book provides a clear step-by-step guide to identifying job opportunities, writing successful application letters, preparing for interviews and being selected. 'A valuable book.' *Teachers Weekly.* 'Cheerful and appropriate . . . particularly helpful in providing checklists designed to bring system to searching for a job. This relaxed, friendly and very helpful little book could bring lasting benefit.' *Times Educational Supplement.* 'Clear and concise . . . should be mandatory reading by all trainees.' *Comlon Magazine (LCCI).* Joan Fletcher is an experienced Manager and Student Counsellor.

112pp. illus. 1 85703 380 9. 4th edition.

BUILDING SELF-ESTEEM
How to replace self-doubt with confidence and well-being

William Stewart

Low self-esteem results from our attaching negative values to ourselves. Its effects are critical and influence almost every aspect of our lives. High self-esteem is positive. It is linked to optimism and the ability to exert some control over events. People who improve their self-esteem find that their lives take on new meaning as confidence grows and well-being is enhanced. This practical, self-help book reveals how the ravages of faulty beliefs about self can be reversed, enabling the reader to develop a firm belief in his or her attributes, accomplishments and abilities. Through a series of exercises and case studies it provides strategies for building self-esteem; it will help readers set clear goals and work steadily towards them. *Building Self-Esteem* is also a valuable handbook for those who work in healthcare and counselling. William Stewart is a freelance counsellor, supervisor and author. His background is in nursing, psychiatric social work and four years as a student counsellor and lecturer at a London college of nursing.

160pp. illus. 1 85703 251 9.

APPLYING FOR A JOB
How to sell your skills and experience to a prospective employer

Judith Johnstone

Tough new realities have hit the jobs market. It is no longer enough to send employers mass-produced letters and CVs with vague details of 'hobbies and interests'. Employers want to know: 'What skills have you got? How much personal commitment? Will it be worth training you in the longer term?' Whether you are a school or college leaver, a mature returner, out of work or facing redundancy, this book shows you step-by-step how to tackle job applications, how to decide what you are really offering, and how to sell this effectively to your future employer. The latest edition has been further revised and updated. 'Very practical and informative.' *Phoenix (Association of Graduate Careers Advisory Services)*. Judith Johnstone is a qualified local government administrator and Member of the Institute of Personnel & Development. She has written extensively on employment topics.

160pp. illus. 1 85703 245 4. 4th edition.

HOW TO GET INTO RADIO
Starting your career as a radio broadcaster

Bernie Simmons

We are about to see a huge expansion in radio stations, and digital audio broadcasting is set to revolutionise the industry. Radio broadcasting now offers an established career path, with industry-approved qualifications like NVQs and university degrees in radio broadcasting. There has never been a more exciting time to make a career in radio. But how do you get in? Where do you get started? What training is on offer? All this and more is revealed in this readable and up-to-the-minute book. 'Useful to any aspiring jock – contains a lot of good advice.' *The Stage & Television Today*. 'Packs a lot in.' *The Music Factory*. Bernie Simmons is a professional radio broadcaster with a wealth of varied experience. He himself started out in nightclub DJ-ing, hospital radio, and in-store radio. He has since worked on breakfast shows on independent local radio, news magazines and phone-in programmes on community radio, worldwide radio services such as BFBS Radio and The BBC World Service, Gold AM Radio and the pioneering Satellite Radio.

153pp. illus. 1 85703 143 1.

How To Books

How To Books provide practical help on a large range of topics. They are available through all good bookshops or can be ordered direct from the distributors. Just tick the titles you want and complete the form on the following page.

___ Apply to an Industrial Tribunal (£7.99)
___ Applying for a Job (£8.99)
___ Applying for a United States Visa (£15.99)
___ Backpacking Round Europe (£8.99)
___ Be a Freelance Journalist (£8.99)
___ Be a Freelance Secretary (£8.99)
___ Become a Freelance Sales Agent (£9.99)
___ Becoming a Father (£8.99)
___ Buy & Run a Shop (£8.99)
___ Buy & Run a Small Hotel (£8.99)
___ Buying a Personal Computer (£9.99)
___ Career Networking (£8.99)
___ Career Planning for Women (£8.99)
___ Cash from your Computer (£9.99)
___ Choosing a Nursing Home (£9.99)
___ Choosing a Package Holiday (£8.99)
___ Claim State Benefits (£9.99)
___ Collecting a Debt (£9.99)
___ Communicate at Work (£7.99)
___ Conduct Staff Appraisals (£7.99)
___ Conducting Effective Interviews (£8.99)
___ Coping with Self Assessment (£9.99)
___ Copyright & Law for Writers (£8.99)
___ Counsel People at Work (£7.99)
___ Creating a Twist in the Tale (£8.99)
___ Creative Writing (£9.99)
___ Critical Thinking for Students (£8.99)
___ Dealing with a Death in the Family (£9.99)
___ Do Your Own Advertising (£8.99)
___ Do Your Own PR (£8.99)
___ Doing Business Abroad (£10.99)
___ Doing Business on the Internet (£12.99)
___ Doing Voluntary Work Abroad (£9.99)
___ Emigrate (£9.99)
___ Employ & Manage Staff (£8.99)
___ Find Temporary Work Abroad (£8.99)
___ Finding a Job in Canada (£9.99)
___ Finding a Job in Computers (£8.99)
___ Finding a Job in New Zealand (£9.99)
___ Finding a Job with a Future (£8.99)
___ Finding Work Overseas (£9.99)
___ Freelance DJ-ing (£8.99)
___ Freelance Teaching & Tutoring (£9.99)
___ Get a Job Abroad (£10.99)
___ Get a Job in Europe (£9.99)
___ Get a Job in France (£9.99)
___ Get a Job in Travel & Tourism (£8.99)
___ Get into Radio (£8.99)
___ Getting a Job in America (£10.99)
___ Getting a Job in Australia (£9.99)
___ Getting into Films & Television (£10.99)
___ Getting That Job (£8.99)
___ Getting your First Job (£8.99)
___ Going to University (£8.99)
___ Having a Baby (£8.99)

___ Helping your Child to Read (£8.99)
___ How to Study & Learn (£8.99)
___ Investing in People (£9.99)
___ Investing in Stocks & Shares (£9.99)
___ Keep Business Accounts (£7.99)
___ Know Your Rights at Work (£8.99)
___ Learning to Counsel (£9.99)
___ Live & Work in Germany (£9.99)
___ Live & Work in Greece (£9.99)
___ Live & Work in Italy (£8.99)
___ Live & Work in Portugal (£9.99)
___ Live & Work in the Gulf (£9.99)
___ Living & Working in America (£12.99)
___ Living & Working in Australia (£12.99)
___ Living & Working in Britain (£8.99)
___ Living & Working in China (£9.99)
___ Living & Working in Hong Kong (£10.99)
___ Living & Working in Israel (£10.99)
___ Living & Work in New Zealand (£9.99)
___ Living & Working in Saudi Arabia (£12.99)
___ Living & Working in the Netherlands (£9.99)
___ Living Away From Home (£8.99)
___ Making a Complaint (£8.99)
___ Making a Video (£9.99)
___ Making a Wedding Speech (£8.99)
___ Manage a Sales Team (£8.99)
___ Manage an Office (£8.99)
___ Manage Computers at Work (£8.99)
___ Manage People at Work (£8.99)
___ Manage Your Career (£8.99)
___ Managing Budgets & Cash Flows (£9.99)
___ Managing Credit (£8.99)
___ Managing Meetings (£8.99)
___ Managing Projects (£8.99)
___ Managing Your Personal Finances (£8.99)
___ Managing Yourself (£8.99)
___ Market Yourself (£8.99)
___ Mastering Book-Keeping (£8.99)
___ Mastering Business English (£8.99)
___ Master GCSE Accounts (£8.99)
___ Master Public Speaking (£8.99)
___ Migrating to Canada (£12.99)
___ Obtaining Visas & Work Permits (£9.99)
___ Organising Effective Training (£9.99)
___ Passing Exams Without Anxiety (£8.99)
___ Passing That Interview (£8.99)
___ Plan a Wedding (£8.99)
___ Planning Your Gap Year (£8.99)
___ Preparing a Business Plan (£8.99)
___ Publish a Book (£9.99)
___ Publish a Newsletter (£9.99)
___ Raise Funds & Sponsorship (£7.99)
___ Rent & Buy Property in France (£9.99)
___ Rent & Buy Property in Italy (£9.99)
___ Research Methods (£8.99)

How To Books

___ Retire Abroad (£8.99)	___ Winning Consumer Competitions (£8.99)
___ Return to Work (£7.99)	___ Winning Presentations (£8.99)
___ Run a Voluntary Group (£8.99)	___ Work from Home (£8.99)
___ Setting up Home in Florida (£9.99)	___ Work in an Office (£7.99)
___ Setting Up Your Own Limited Company (£9.99)	___ Work in Retail (£8.99)
	___ Work with Dogs (£8.99)
___ Spending a Year Abroad (£8.99)	___ Working Abroad (£14.99)
___ Start a Business from Home (£7.99)	___ Working as a Holiday Rep (£9.99)
___ Start a New Career (£6.99)	___ Working as an Au Pair (£8.99)
___ Starting to Manage (£8.99)	___ Working in Japan (£10.99)
___ Starting to Write (£8.99)	___ Working in Photography (£8.99)
___ Start Word Processing (£8.99)	___ Working in the Gulf (£10.99)
___ Start Your Own Business (£8.99)	___ Working in Hotels & Catering (£9.99)
___ Study Abroad (£8.99)	___ Working on Contract Worldwide (£9.99)
___ Study & Live in Britain (£7.99)	___ Working on Cruise Ships (£9.99)
___ Studying at University (£8.99)	___ Write a Press Release (£9.99)
___ Studying for a Degree (£8.99)	___ Write & Sell Computer Software (£9.99)
___ Successful Grandparenting (£8.99)	___ Write for Television (£8.99)
___ Successful Mail Order Marketing (£9.99)	___ Writing a CV that Works (£8.99)
___ Successful Single Parenting (£8.99)	___ Writing a Non Fiction Book (£9.99)
___ Survive Divorce (£8.99)	___ Writing a Report (£8.99)
___ Surviving Redundancy (£8.99)	___ Writing a Textbook (£12.99)
___ Taking in Students (£8.99)	___ Writing an Assignment (£8.99)
___ Taking on Staff (£8.99)	___ Writing an Essay (£8.99)
___ Taking Your A-Levels (£8.99)	___ Writing & Publishing Poetry (£9.99)
___ Teach Abroad (£8.99)	___ Writing & Selling a Novel (£8.99)
___ Teach Adults (£8.99)	___ Writing Business Letters (£8.99)
___ Teaching Someone to Drive (£8.99)	___ Writing for Publication (£8.99)
___ Travel Round the World (£8.99)	___ Writing Reviews (£9.99)
___ Understand Finance at Work (£8.99)	___ Writing Romantic Fiction (£9.99)
___ Use a Library (£7.99)	___ Writing Science Fiction (£9.99)
___ Using the Internet (£9.99)	___ Writing Your Dissertation (£8.99)

To: Plymbridge Distributors Ltd, Plymbridge House, Estover Road, Plymouth PL6 7PZ. Customer Services Tel: (01752) 202301. Fax: (01752) 202331.

Please send me copies of the titles I have indicated. Please add postage & packing (UK £1, Europe including Eire, £2, World £3 airmail).

☐ I enclose cheque/PO payable to Plymbridge Distributors Ltd for £ _____

☐ Please charge to my ☐ MasterCard, ☐ Visa, ☐ AMEX card.

Account No. ☐☐☐☐☐☐☐☐☐☐☐☐

Card Expiry Date ☐☐ 19 ☎ **Credit Card orders may be faxed or phoned.**

Customer Name (CAPITALS) ....

Address ....

.... Postcode ....

Telephone .... Signature ....

Every effort will be made to despatch your copy as soon as possible but to avoid possible disappointment please allow up to 21 days for despatch time (42 days if overseas). Prices and availability are subject to change without notice.

Code BPA